Lynne Palmer's

YOUR
LUCKY DAYS
AND
NUMBERS

D1598569

YOUR LUCKY DAYS AND NUMBERS

Copyright © 1981 by Lynne Palmer

All rights reserved worldwide. This is copyrighted material. No part of this book may be used or reproduced in any form or by any electronic mechanical means, including information storage or retrieval systems without permission in writing from Lynne Palmer and Star Bright Publishers. Anyone being requested to reproduce all or part of this book should contact the publisher immediately at (702) 369-4026 to verify authorization by the copyright owner. Failure to confirm authorization before printing will result in increased liability and damages. Any infringement of these rights and/or removal of any copyright notices by publishers, printers, marketing companies or others will be prosecuted to the full extend of the law.

FIRST PRINTING April 1998

ISBN 0-9652296-8-8

Library of Congress Catalogue Number 98-90169

Published by:

STAR BRIGHT PUBLISHERS
2235 EAST FLAMINGO ROAD
SUITE 300-D
LAS VEGAS, NV 89119

Printed and bound in the United States of America

BOOKS BY LYNNE PALMER

Astrological Almanac (annual)

Do-It-Yourself Publicity Directory

Astrological Compatibility

Prosperity Signs

Signs for Success

Is Your Name Lucky For You"

Nixon's Horoscope

Horoscope of Billy Rose

ABC Chart Erection

ABC Major Progressions

ABC Basic Chart Reading

Pluto Ephermeris (1900-2000)

Money Magic

Astro-Guide to Nutrition and Vitamins

Gambling to Win

The Astrological Treasure Map

CONTENTS

Gloria Swanson
87W39 41N52
March 27, 1899 12:20 AM CST

ASTRODYNES

		Totals			Astrodyne Components					
PLANETS	Power	%	Harmony	House	Dignity	MR	Aspects	Harmony	Discord	Neutral
Saturn	80.08	13.2	-29.49	14.82	0.00	0.00	65.86	17.64	-47.13	29.40
Neptune	75.85	12.4	-13.39	14.40	-3.00	5.00	61.45	24.61	-38.00	30.60
Mercury	69.24	11.4	5.19	13.12	0.00	0.00	56.12	33.57	-28.38	17.32
ASC	51.56	8.5	-9.16	15.00	0.00	0.00	36.56	12.33	-21.49	19.29
Uranus	50.28	8.2	2.39	9.05	-3.00	5.00	41.23	21.29	-18.90	20.27
Venus	49.24	8.1	31.81	8.17	1.00	0.00	41.07	37.42	-5.61	14.53
Pluto	47.52	7.8	2.01	6.67	0.00	0.00	40.85	14.86	-12.85	20.91
Jupiter	42.86	7.0	11.02	13.08	-1.00	5.00	29.78	21.84	-10.82	20.07
MC	42.16	6.9	2.24	15.00	0.00	0.00	27.16	12.07	-9.83	20.54
Mars	35.03	5.7	-18.11	12.66	-3.00	5.00	22.37	6.54	-24.65	16.03
MOON	33.01	5.4	-6.08	9.43	0.00	0.00	23.58	6.32	-12.40	14.97
SUN	32.61	5.3	-7.81	7.60	3.00	0.00	25.01	10.11	-17.92	7.93
Total	610.04	100%	-29.38							

HOUSES	Power	%	Harmony
First	153.67	16.1	-33.14
Seventh	145.50	15.2	-28.91
Tenth	109.64	11.5	29.16
Second	106.95	11.1	13.69
Fourth	86.75	9.1	-3.86
Sixth	82.14	8.6	4.60
Twelfth	71.71	7.5	7.90
Ninth	67.63	7.1	-3.49
Third	62.28	6.5	-8.40
Eighth	24.65	2.6	-4.99
Fifth	24.62	2.4	15.90
Eleventh	20.63	2.2	-4.02

SIGNS	Power	%	Harmony
Sagittarius	225.38	23.6	-25.24
Gemini	192.61	20.2	-6.19
Aries	119.36	12.5	-11.67
Libra	99.79	10.4	12.06
Aquarius	65.61	6.9	28.43
Scorpio	63.49	6.6	7.00
Cancer	51.53	5.4	-21.15
Capricorn	40.34	4.2	-14.74
Virgo	34.62	3.6	2.59
Pisces	29.67	3.1	-0.59
Taurus	24.62	2.6	15.90
Leo	8.15	0.9	-1.95

-SUMMARY-

	Power	%	Harmony
Private	393.61	41.2	-19.95
Friendship	339.01	35.5	-12.27
Community	222.65	23.3	18.86
Success	297.33	31.2	47.45
Vitality	245.90	25.7	-20.13
Relationship	228.41	20.9	-41.30
Intuition	180.11	19.2	-0.95

-SUMMARY-

	Power	%	Harmony
Mutable	482.28	50.5	-29.43
Movable	311.02	32.6	-35.50
Fixed	161.87	16.9	49.58
Air	358.01	37.5	34.30
Fire	352.89	36.9	-38.86
Water	144.69	15.1	-14.74
Earth	99.68	10.4	3.75

6

INTRODUCTION

I'll bet you have heard people say, "I wish I were lucky", "I just ran out of Luck", "The dice are cold; it's time to quit", or "Lady Luck's not smiling at me tonight." Are you aware that you can control your luck? Why waste valuable money gambling at the wrong time? Do you know that there are days, according to Astrology and Numerology that are far more favorable than others?

The science of Numerology has been effectively used for centuries by royalty, celebrities and the general public. By using Numerology, you save time and money; you thus avoid headaches and mistakes that could prove costly both financially and emotionally. You should NOT gamble (or as much) on unfavorable days because Lady Luck may not be with you. However on the favorable days you may wind up a winner! Gambling includes Lotto, the lottery, bingo, cards, horse racing, jai-alai, raffle and sweepstakes tickets, greyhound racing, point spreads in football, boxing, fights, basketball and baseball, in casinos and anything else that is speculative, such as the stock, options, futures, warrants, or commodities markets, or opening a business.

In this book, you'll learn how to use PERSONAL NUMEROLOGY for your daily, monthly and yearly forecasts. It is based upon the Universal Year (the Calendar Year the world is in currently) and YOUR birthday (day and month). A Universal Year starts on January first of every year, and the number it corresponds to indicates your personal, as well as world, conditions for that particular year, i.e., 1986 equates to a six year for the universe --- a six year signifies reconstruction. Thus, in the U.S.A. the tax

7

reform reconstructing is a good example of how this works on a country level. 1987 equates to a seven year for the universe --- a seven year brings about an interest in religion and spiritual matters (we had religious scandals in 1987), travel and promotional endeavors. 1988 equates to an eight year --- money flourishes worldwide. 1989 equates to a nine year --- endings, the end of an era which we saw. 1990 equates to a one year --- new beginnings, i.e., the establishment of the Eastern countries in Europe and their independence. 1991 equates to a two year --- changes; thus we had global changes in the Eastern countries - The Soviet Union and Yugoslavia - and the independent states that evolved and the ouster of communism. These changes affected governments and the public in both business and personal ways. 1992 equates to a three year --- socializing, peace, travel, recreation and business expansion. The European borders opened up. It is a time to relax, enjoy life, and make and spend money.

Once you have learned about your Personal Year, Month and Day, you will learn how to use that information to your advantage. It can aid you in your daily life, and you could then plan ahead when to take action. You can combine Personal Numerology with another form of Numerology that employs Astrology. Each sign of the zodiac and planets vibrate to a specific number. Through the mathematics of Astrodynes, you can discover whether a sign or planet is harmonious in your horoscope. You can then take the number it corresponds to and the result is YOUR LUCKY NUMBER! Or perhaps you have many lucky numbers! If this is the case, one will be stronger and luckier than the other(s) because that one number will have more power; this harmonious power is measured by Astrodynes.

Your lucky numbers can be used for gambling and just about everything else. For instance, before you buy or rent a house, office, store or apartment, select a number that has a fortunate influence on you. Or make sure your telephone number and automobile license plate vibrate to a harmonious number. Borrow money in amounts that are lucky for you. There are countless ways to use numbers to your advantage.

Have your ever thought that you lost at the race track because it was an unlucky day to gamble, or that you did not choose the right post position, race or jockey number? Did you every borrow money that was difficult to repay? Perhaps you took the loan at the wrong time or the amount you borrowed was not a lucky sum (number) for you! And now, with this book, perhaps you will have the answers you have been waiting for. Good Luck.

CHAPTER ONE
NUMEROLOGY TABLES FOR YOUR
PERSONAL YEARS, MONTHS, DAYS

In this Chapter, you will *first* find your *Individual* Number listed on pages 11-14. Once you know this number, you will then be able to ascertain your Personal *Year* Number. Once you have discovered your Personal *Year* Number, you will be able to find your Personal *Month* Number. Once you have ascertained your Personal *Month* Number, you will be able to know your Personal Day *Number*. Once you have discovered your Personal Year, Month or Day Number, read Chapter Two, and interpret the meanings of these numbers and how you can apply them in your life --- especially if you want to get rich quickly!

FINDING YOUR INDIVIDUAL NUMBER
1.   Find your birth date on the Individual Number Table that follows (Pages 11-14.).
2.   On the Individual Number Table (pages 11-14), across from your birth date is a corresponding number called your Individual Number. Once you know your individual Number, you will be able to ascertain your Personal Year Number by reading page 15.

INDIVIDUAL NUMBER TABLE

January Individual Day Number	February Individual Day Number	March Individual Day Number
1 = 2	1 = 3	1 = 4
2 = 3	2 = 4	2 = 5
3 = 4	3 = 5	3 = 6
4 = 5	4 = 6	4 = 7
5 = 6	5 = 7	5 = 8
6 = 7	6 = 8	6 = 9
7 = 8	7 = 9	7 = 1
8 = 9	8 = 1	8 = 2
9 = 1	9 = 2	9 = 3
10 = 2	10 = 3	10 = 4
11 = 3	11 = 4	11 = 5
12 = 4	12 = 5	12 = 6
13 = 5	13 = 6	13 = 7
14 = 6	14 = 7	14 = 8
15 = 7	15 = 8	15 = 9
16 = 8	16 = 9	16 = 1
17 = 9	17 = 1	17 = 2
18 = 1	18 = 2	18 = 3
19 = 2	19 = 3	19 = 4
20 = 3	20 = 4	20 = 5
21 = 4	21 = 5	21 = 6
22 = 5	22 = 6	22 = 7
23 = 6	23 = 7	23 = 8
24 = 7	24 = 8	24 = 9
25 = 8	25 = 9	25 = 1
26 = 9	26 = 1	26 = 2
27 = 1	27 = 2	27 = 3
28 = 2	28 = 3	28 = 4
29 = 3	29 = 4	29 = 5
30 = 4		30 = 6
31 = 5		31 = 7

INDIVIDUAL NUMBER TABLE

April Individual Day Number	May Individual Day Number	June Individual Day Number
1 = 5	1 = 6	1 = 7
2 = 6	2 = 7	2 = 8
3 = 7	3 = 8	3 = 9
4 = 8	4 = 9	4 = 1
5 = 9	5 = 1	5 = 2
6 = 1	6 = 2	6 = 3
7 = 2	7 = 3	7 = 4
8 = 3	8 = 4	8 = 5
9 = 4	9 = 5	9 = 6
10 = 5	10 = 6	10 = 7
11 = 6	11 = 7	11 = 8
12 = 7	12 = 8	12 = 9
13 = 8	13 = 9	13 = 1
14 = 9	14 = 1	14 = 2
15 = 1	15 = 2	15 = 3
16 = 2	16 = 3	16 = 4
17 = 3	17 = 4	17 = 5
18 = 4	18 = 5	18 = 6
19 = 5	19 = 6	19 = 7
20 = 6	20 = 7	20 = 8
21 = 7	21 = 8	21 = 9
22 = 8	22 = 9	22 = 1
23 = 9	23 = 1	23 = 2
24 = 1	24 = 2	24 = 3
25 = 2	25 = 3	25 = 4
26 = 3	26 = 4	26 = 5
27 = 4	27 = 5	27 = 6
28 = 5	28 = 6	28 = 7
29 = 6	29 = 7	29 = 8
30 = 7	30 = 8	30 = 9
	31 = 9	

INDIVIDUAL NUMBER TABLE

July Individual Day Number	August Individual Day Number	September Individual Day Number
1 = 8	1 = 9	1 = 1
2 = 9	2 = 1	2 = 2
3 = 1	3 = 2	3 = 3
4 = 2	4 = 3	4 = 4
5 = 3	5 = 4	5 = 5
6 = 4	6 = 5	6 = 6
7 = 5	7 = 6	7 = 7
8 = 6	8 = 7	8 = 8
9 = 7	9 = 8	9 = 9
10 = 8	10 = 9	10 = 1
11 = 9	11 = 1	11 = 2
12 = 1	12 = 2	12 = 3
13 = 2	13 = 3	13 = 4
14 = 3	14 = 4	14 = 5
15 = 4	15 = 5	15 = 6
16 = 5	16 = 6	16 = 7
17 = 6	17 = 7	17 = 8
18 = 7	18 = 8	18 = 9
19 = 8	19 = 9	19 = 1
20 = 9	20 = 1	20 = 2
21 = 1	21 = 2	21 = 3
22 = 2	22 = 3	22 = 4
23 = 3	23 = 4	23 = 5
24 = 4	24 = 5	24 = 6
25 = 5	25 = 6	25 = 7
26 = 6	26 = 7	26 = 8
27 = 7	27 = 8	27 = 9
28 = 8	28 = 9	28 = 1
29 = 9	29 = 1	29 = 2
30 = 1	30 = 2	30 = 3
31 = 2	31 = 3	

INDIVIDUAL NUMBER TABLE

October Individual Day Number	November Individual Day Number	December Individual Day Number
1 = 2	1 = 3	1 = 4
2 = 3	2 = 4	2 = 5
3 = 4	3 = 5	3 = 6
4 = 5	4 = 6	4 = 7
5 = 6	5 = 7	5 = 8
6 = 7	6 = 8	6 = 9
7 = 8	7 = 9	7 = 1
8 = 9	8 = 1	8 = 2
9 = 1	9 = 2	9 = 3
10 = 2	10 = 3	10 = 4
11 = 3	11 = 4	11 = 5
12 = 4	12 = 5	12 = 6
13 = 5	13 = 6	13 = 7
14 = 6	14 = 7	14 = 8
15 = 7	15 = 8	15 = 9
16 = 8	16 = 9	16 = 1
17 = 9	17 = 1	17 = 2
18 = 1	18 = 2	18 = 3
19 = 2	19 = 3	19 = 4
20 = 3	20 = 4	20 = 5
21 = 4	21 = 5	21 = 6
22 = 5	22 = 6	22 = 7
23 = 6	23 = 7	23 = 8
24 = 7	24 = 8	24 = 9
25 = 8	25 = 9	25 = 1
26 = 9	26 = 1	26 = 2
27 = 1	27 = 2	27 = 3
28 = 2	28 = 3	28 = 4
29 = 3	29 = 4	29 = 5
30 = 4	30 = 5	30 = 6
31 = 5		31 = 7

TO FIND YOUR PERSONAL YEAR NUMBER

All numbers in the Personal Year, Month and Day branch of Numerology go from 1 to 9; therefore, any number that is more than 9 is broken down to a single digit number.

A.

Every year has a different number it vibrates to - from 1 to 9, and it is repeated again. The numbers for that year are added and the result is called the Universal Year Number. To obtain your PERSONAL YEAR NUMBER, you must first ascertain the Universal Year Number. Refer to Table of Years given on page 16.

Example: If you want to know your Personal Year Number for 1987, you must first add the numbers that make up for 1987. 1 + 9 + 8 + 7 = 25. The 25 is more than 9; therefore, break it down to a single digit number by adding the number that make up 25 (2 + 5 = 7); the result is the Universal Number for the year 1987, which is 7.

B.

Add your Individual Number (found on pages 11-14) to the Universal Year Number (see Table of Years, page 16), and the result is your Personal Year Number. Once you know your Personal Year Number, you will be able to ascertain your Personal Month Number. However, if you want to read the interpretation of the Personal Year you are in read Chapter Two.

Example: Your birthday is June 25th, 1987, and you want to know your Personal Year Number for 1987:

Individual Number   4
Universal Number for 1987 = $\underline{+\,7}$
                                       11

Since (11) is more than 9, 11 must be broken down to a single digit. Number 11 is 1 + 1 = 2; therefore, 2 is your Personal Year

Number for the year 1987. This is followed by 3 for 1988, 4 for 1989, 5 for 1990, 6 for 1991, 7 for 1992, 8 for 1993, 9 for 1994, 1 for 1995, (remember, it starts back to one after nine), and 2 for 1996...and so on.

Table of Years

Calendar Year	Universal Year	Calendar Year	Universal Year	Calendar Year	Universal Year
1987 = 7		1994 = 5		2001 = 3	
1988 = 8		1995 = 6		2002 = 4	
1989 = 9		1996 = 7		2003 = 5	
1990 = 1		1997 = 8		2004 = 6	
1991 = 2		1998 = 9		2005 = 7	
1992 = 3		1999 = 1		2006 = 8	
1993 = 4		2000 = 2		2007 = 9	

To Find Your Personal Month Number

In Personal Month Numerology, all months equal a number as follows:

not the year of your birth:. use only the year you're interested in.

Month Table

January	=	1 (the first month)
February	=	2 (the second month)
March	=	3 (the third month)
April	=	4 (the fourth month)
May	=	5 (the fifth month)
June	=	6 (the sixth month)
July	=	7 (the seventh month)
August	=	8 (the eighth month)
September	=	9 (the ninth month)
October	=	1 (the tenth month is more than 9; therefore, break it down to a single digit number by dropping the 0...; therefore October is one month).
November	=	2 (the eleventh month is more than 9; therefore, break it down to a single digit number by adding the 11 in the eleventh month, i.e. 1 + 1 = 2).
December	=	3 (the twelfth month, is more than 9; therefore, break it down to a single digit number by adding the 12 in the twelfth month, i.e., 1 + 2 = 3).

A.

Find the Month Number from the preceding Month Table (page 17). The month signifies the month you are interested in knowing about.

B.

Add your Personal Year Number to the Month Number and the result is your Personal Month Number. (Once you know your Personal Month Number you will be able to ascertain your Personal Day Number). If you want to read the interpretation of the Personal Month, read Chapter Two.

Example: Your birthday is June 25th, your Personal Year Number for 1987 is 2 and you want to know your Personal Month Number for December 1987:

$$\begin{aligned}
\text{Personal Year Number} &= 2 \\
\text{Personal Month Number} &= \underline{+\ 3} \\
\text{Personal Month Number} & \\
\text{for December 1987} &= 5
\end{aligned}$$

To Find Your Personal Day Number
A.

Find the Day Number. The day signifies day you are interested in knowing about. The first day of the month is 1, the second day is 2, the ninth day is 9, the tenth day is 1. (Drop the zero, 10 becomes 1 because it is more than the 9 and must be broken down to a single digit number). The fourteenth (14) is broken down to a single digit number and becomes 5 (1 + 4 = 5), and so on with all the days of the month.

B.

Add your Personal Month Number to the Day Number and the result is your Personal Day Number. However, if you want to read the interpretation of the Personal Day you are in, read Chapter Two.

18

Example: Your birthday is June 25th, your Personal Year Number for 1987 is 2, your Personal Month Number for December 1987 is 5, and you want to know your Personal Day Number for December 14, 1987:

> December 1987 Personal
> Month Number   =   5
> December 14 is broken
> down to a single digit
> (it is more than 9);
> therefore, 1 + 4 = 5   = +5
>   10

Break the 10 down to a single digit number (drop the 0). Your Personal Day Number for December 14, 1987 is 1 (one).

CHAPTER TWO
INTERPRETATION OF YOUR PERSONAL YEARS, MONTHS, AND DAYS

THE FOLLOWING NUMBERS APPLY TO YOUR PERSONAL YEAR, MONTH AND/OR DAY. IF YOU ARE IN A TWO YEAR, MONTH OR DAY - READ TWO. IF YOU ARE IN A NINE YEAR MONTH OR DAY - READ NINE. AND SO FORTH AND SO ON FOR THE REMAINING NUMBERS. ALSO, REFER TO "TIPS AND HINTS" WHICH FOLLOW THE NUMBERS ONE THROUGH NINE.

ONE

This is the time to start anything new or bring out something (book, movie, video, etc.) new. Always *start* projects when you are in a One. Do not gamble. Invest. Move. Marry. Date someone for the first time. Expand a business, etc. Start (take) legal action. Shop. Express ideas. Form new associations. Go on interviews. Get publicity. Make decisions. Ask for a raise. Socialize. Give, or go to, a party. Borrow or lend money. Order clothes or objects from catalogues. See a printer or place an ad. Advertise. Make love to someone new. Take a trip. (Start the journey in a One Day or Month.) Start a new job, profession, hobby or avocation. Purchase or sell property, stocks or other objects, i.e. works of art. Write letters or send correspondence. Compose music, lyrics, or be an author or start a painting (if you are an artist). Apply for credit, insurance, Social Security or a pension. Make important appointments. Your energy is fantastic!

Romance: When you meet a person for the first time and you are in a Number 1 Day, the relationship can get off to a good start because One signifies "new beginnings". However, if you are already involved with someone, then a Number 1 Day is a wonderful time to do new things, such as go to a different restaurant to dine in, or go to the park, ballet, opera or museum. Or go bowling, take a trip to a new town or make love in a different way or location. The preceding also applies if you are in a One Month or Year.

TWO

Watch out for deceit, lies, changes of plans (as they may be your doing or others'), cancellations, delays and confusion. An indecisive period. People tell you one thing and do another, or *you* may make plans on another day, and when the Two day arrives, *you* change your mind. Everything seems to move slowly. Be patient, diplomatic and tactful. It is not a good time to go on interviews, auditions, to shop, or to borrow or lend money. It is not a favorable time to marry or get engaged. You could move or change a job without too much mishap. Don't take legal action, make decisions, ask for a raise or make important appointments. Do not invest when you are in a Two Year, Month, or Day; otherwise, it may go sour and cost you heavy financial losses. Don't form partnerships; you can't trust others, but you might do so and later regret it. You can win at gambling, Two involves changes. Therefore, a change occurs when you win the jackpot on a slot machine, or huge sums of money on table games or sports betting. Or what about the lottery? If you win big bucks, changes are in store for you. Do not believe in the promises of others or all that is offered at this time.

Romance: If you meet a person for the first time, you may be interested at that moment, only to change your mind later. Romance is slow in getting started and nothing may come of it. However, if it is a romance that has been on-going, a Two day can be mesmerizing. If you've been dating, but have not yet had sex, you could have it in on a Two Day - because that is the day of

21

changes. The preceding also applies if you are in a Two Month or Year.

THREE

Gamble. Invest. Move. Expand a business. Shop. Borrow or lend money. Socialize. Give, or go to parties. Travel. Start projects. Go to court; start a law suit or settle one. Go on interviews. Get publicity. Money may come in and go out just as quickly. You must take care that you don't goof off - wasting time and being lazy. The desire to live it up and have the time of your life makes it difficult to concentrate on work. People tend to be nicer than usual to you when you are in a Three period. Get pregnant. Ask for a raise. Auditions are favored. Marry. Date someone for the first time. Make important appointments.

Romance: When you are in a Three Day, Month or Year, you have fun, a lot of laughs and the social scene sparkles like champagne. Friends are wonderful to be with, and the more company the better; however, you may prefer to be alone with a loved one. This is a time of companionship, hugs, kisses, embraces, and warm, tender and affectionate moments. Sex is beautiful and romantic. It is a sensuous time.

FOUR

Do not invest, borrow or lend money, expand a business, marry or date someone for the first time. This is a laborious period and you are loaded down with work which, at the moment, has seemingly little rewards. Rest, eat properly and get a health checkup. You may feel tired all, or most of, the time. This is a favorable time to update machinery, organize, decorate, buy real estate and work hard. Tend to business and keep your nose to the grindstone, because you'll experience the benefits on the following day, month, or year (depending if you are in a Four Year, Month or Day). It is best to avoid games of chance, taking

22

risks and all forms of speculation, including gambling. However, if you must indulge, be thrifty and spend only a bare minimum. Try to save money for a better time.

Romance: It is a difficult time for romance; usually a person is not as interested in affairs of the heart because the energy is directed toward work, business and/or a career. You may feel too tired for sex or find it laborious and sapping your strength. This is a time when you may prefer making money.

FIVE

Favorable to gamble, invest, move, socialize, travel, expand a business, go on interviews, audition, get publicity, borrow or lend money. Apply for credit, insurance, Social Security or a pension. Make important appointments. Ask for a raise or favor. Start new projects. Change jobs, your avocation or profession. Indulge in a hobby. Take legal action or settle in or out of court. Express ideas. Be creative. Advertise. Buy or sell stocks, property or works of art. New opportunities and unexpected changes are favored. Do not overindulge, go shopping or be impulsive. Be careful of accidents. Women may have difficulty with the menstrual period or have female problems. Be ready for shocks, upheavals and surprises. This is a lucky and happy period even though some things may be upsetting.

Romance: Date someone new for the first time. Marry. When you are in a number Five day, month or year, romance is intriguing. A new person may weave a magic spell and you may be so mesmerized that you do not know what you are doing when you are with that fascinating individual. This hypnotic state may be difficult to break - and you may want it to last forever. However, this is a period of surprises; although the person could be a permanent fixture, he or she may wind up as just a passing, but unforgettable memory. During this time, your sexual nature is

23

aroused to the point where you may entertain, or actually participate in kinky, strange, unusual sex. This is the time to experiment. Sex is wild!

SIX

Do not gamble. Invest, go on interviews and auditions. Go on a tour. Shop. Move. Marry. Divorce. Date. Collect and pay debts (especially long-standing ones). Take care of duties. Get publicity. Borrow or lend money. Redecorate, clean house and drawers. Do your "spring cleaning". Buy real estate. This is a great time to reorganize papers, the house and to restructure your life. Take on added responsibilities. An interest in the family makes you protective of others. Form long-lasting relationships.

Romance: When you are in a Six day, month or year, romance is quiet and enjoyable. There is a feeling of protectiveness and a desire to take care of the other person. Duty, responsibility, food, shelter and a family are uppermost in your mind. Marriage is thought about and companionship is highly desired. If you are already married, these thoughts are strengthened toward your mate. Lovemaking is warm, relaxed and beautiful. It is a time of mating.

SEVEN

Do not gamble unless you spend only a bare minimum and wait for a more favorable time to take risks. Don't invest, borrow or lend money, shop, expand or start a new business. Try to avoid an operation if it can be done. This is a time when you may be alone more than usual - it could be your doing or other people just don't seem to be around or get in touch with you. It is a time to meditate and get in touch with your inner self. However, avoid daydreaming. Take action and be careful of indulging in too much fantasy thinking and get-rich-quick schemes. Delegate responsibilities. Promote projects and yourself. Get publicity.

This is a mystical period and you may feel drawn to metaphysical areas. You may wonder why you were born. What is your mission in life? You may become involved in spiritual pursuits and hold a seance.

Romance: You may get married; however, the desire for companionship isn't strong because you may prefer solitude. It is a romantic period, although it may be more in your head than physical. You could fantasize about love and sex. You will tend to be poetical and may want to listen to soft music, have a candlelight supper, hold hands, hug, kiss and look each other in the eyes. It is a spiritual type of relationship; therefore, you may feel as if a psychic bond existed between the two of you.

EIGHT

Gamble. Invest. Expand. Date. Marry. Change jobs. Get publicity. Go on interviews. Start a new business. Grasp opportunities. Take action. Solve problems. Do not shop. Borrow money for business expansion. Avoid being overly generous. You may want to buy gifts for others and treat your friends to lunch and dinner. This is a period to reap the harvest - finances and business flourish. Opportunities to increase your prestige are presented. You work hard, but it pays off. It is very difficult to save money during this period. You just seem to spend and spend, regardless of how much you try to be conservative. Socialize. You may give a party, but avoid splurging. Service given by others is good now. Money seems to go through your hands like water. It is a difficult time to hold on to cash, but you must make an effort to do so because, when you are in a Nine (especially a Nine year), many financial problems may develop. So prepare yourself for the Nine.

Romance: When you are in an Eight day, month or year, you are in the mood to treat your loved one to a good time. You enjoy romantic candlelight suppers with soft music playing in the background. The idea is to wine and dine your beloved. The showering of gifts also takes place. You spend a lot of money, but it is not the price that counts; you are just in a sharing and giving frame of mind. It is done from the heart. It is an affectionate time.

NINE

Do not borrow or lend money. Avoid shopping. Don't expand a business, go on interviews, advertise for the first time, make new purchases or start anything new. You *can make* money in a Nine day, month or year. Gambling is favored; a Nine is ending a situation which winning can do. Avoid risks in business, speculation and any form of new enterprise. Don't bring out a new product, book, movie, video, record, etc. Don't start a new job or change occupations or professions. Get divorced. Separate from a mate, partner or loved one. (It may happen whether you like it or not). This is a period of endings, terminations, frustrations and unexpected expenses. Debts pile up to enormous sums. (They could be carry-over from an Eight day, month or year). People don't seem to help you. You work hard and are easily exhausted. Your energy is down. Watch your health. Cut down on physical activity. Try to rest. Finish projects.

Romance: You may end a relationship, especially if you start it when you are in a Nine period. It is a frustrating time, with many disappointments in the love department. You will feel like ending everything because you are so disgusted with your loved one's behavior. Love can be costly - financially and emotionally. You may say, "I've had all I can take. I am through with _____ ". You don't feel romantic during this time; and if you do indulge in

26

ex, you may feel drained and completely worn out from the xperience.

TIPS AND HINTS

The luckiest Years, Months and Days are when you are in a umber 1, 2, 3, 5, 6 or 8. Socialize on a 1, 3, 5, 6, or 8 day. Also, nese days are favorable for borrowing money. If you are in a Five /ear and January is a Six Month for you, then this is a super time o borrow money. Try to plan your activities so the year, month nd day are simultaneously favorable. If you can't get all three armonious at the same time, at least try to get two of them avorable.

Do not ask for a raise or favor if you are in a 2, 4, 7, or 9 day, nonth or year. There are favorable days to make decisions, ask or a raise, promotion or transfer (numbers 1, 3, 5, 6, 8). It is ossible that if you asked for a raise on an unfavorable day - such s Nine - you could lose your job. If you quit or start a job and/or nitiate a business on an adverse day (number 2, 4, 7 or 9), you nay regret it. It is best to use your favorable days to guarantee our best chance for success. You'll get rich quicker by using hese auspicious days, months and years (numbers 1, 3, 5, 6, 8). Also promote projects, expand a business and/or modernize an ffice/business on any of these lucky dates.

Are you aware that there is a propitious time to go on an nterview and to sign contracts (numbers 1, 3, 5, 6, 8)? If you try o borrow money on an unlucky day (numbers 2, 4, 7, 9), either ou may not get the loan or you might have difficulty repaying it. Therefore, if you apply for the loan on the favorable days numbers 1, 3, 5, 6, 8). On certain days, it is easier to pay your lebts. It's possible in a Nine day, month or year that you could nd your debts, or you may have difficulty getting out of financial dversity. The creditors harass you more than at other times.

27

As for gambling, there are favorable periods (numbers 2, 3, 5, 8, 9); and risky ones, too (numbers 1, 4, 6, 7). Therefore, be thrifty when adverse problems arise. It is to your advantage to know in advance those days when people are deceitful or when delays and changes in plans may occur (a number Two day, month or year). If you marry at the wrong time (number 2, 4, 9), it is possible that it will not last. I know several people who met mates and married in a Nine year and were divorced before the Nine year had ended.

If you shop on a day that is lucky (number 1, 3, 4, 5, 6), you will be thrifty; however, on an unfavorable day (numbers 2, 7, 8, 9) you are inclined to spend money recklessly.

Give parties and take trips on those days when you will enjoy it the most (numbers 1, 2, 3, 5, 7, 8). There are days when you may eat in excess (numbers 2, 4, 6, 8, 9) and wind up gaining weight. If you, or hired help, clean house on a favorable day (number 4 and, especially 6), a neat and thorough job will make your place sparkle; although more time will be spent in the process due to your being too picky - a perfectionist. Therefore, clean house on another day and it will be done in a jiffy; however, it may not be as clean as you would prefer. Work is performed best and the service is at a high when you are in a number 1, 3, 4, 6, or 8 day.

Now that you know about how you are when you are in a particular day, month or year, what about the other person you're involved with? Look up his or her birthday in the Individual Number pages 11-14) and figure his or her Personal Days, Months and Years. You can then pick days when you both have harmonious periods, i.e., you are in a Three day and he/she is in a Five day - because those are favorable days for romance - so have fun! If the person you are dating is in an unfavorable day you will be better equipped to handle the individual; thus, the two of you can be happier because you now understand his/her moods better. The preceding also applies to family and business relationships.

Start to think in what numbered day, month or year you are. Keep a daily track of your personal Numbers and plan your life around these dates, if possible. The result will be a happier, more productive and richer life. Perhaps your luck will be better than ever and maybe you just might be the next multi-million-dollar winner!

CHAPTER THREE
GAMBLING AND NUMEROLOGY

Numerology is applied to all forms of gambling (games of chance, commodities, stocks, bonds - anything that is speculative and a risk, such as backing a Broadway show). Sports (point spreads in football, baseball, basketball, ice hockey, tennis, prize fights), casino gambling (crap games, roulette wheels, blackjack, poker, bingo, slot machines, baccarat), lotto, the lottery, and greyhound, horse and harness racing, and all private gambling between individuals should all be played according to your best day, month and year according to Personal Numerology.

Buy your lottery, lotto or sweepstakes ticket on a favorable date according to Numerology (when you are in a 2, 3, 5, 7, 8, 9) and make sure that the drawing of the ticket is also on one of these days. If these dates are chosen, your chance to be a winner is improved.

Note: You may *not* want to stop gambling just because it is *not* the best time to do so; therefore, on the dates that are NOT lucky for you to gamble (numbers 1, 4, 6), save your money for a day when Lady Luck is smiling in your direction. These dates (numbers 1, 4, 6) may not be the greatest, or bring the big jackpot or make you a millionaire, but it is possible to win small amounts on them. Therefore, on these dates, gamble a bare minimum amount of money. Be practical and save your money for an auspicious day and spend a larger amount of money on the dates that give you the best chance to win (numbers 2, 3, 5, 7, 8, 9).

The LUCKIEST Numerology Personal Year, Month or Day Number for gambling is 5, followed by 8, 3, 2, 9 and 7. Thus, the most unfavorable Numerology Personal Year, Month or Day Number for gambling is 4, followed by 6, then 1. However, as mentioned previously, you can still win when in a 1, 4, or 6 Year, Month or Day. If you are in a Personal Year number 1, 4 or 6 - at least *pick a lucky Personal Month* (number 5, 8, 3, 6, 7 or 2) to gamble. This improves your chances of winning. If you gamble when you are in a Year, Month and Day that are unlucky (numbers 1, 4 or 6), you are likely to lose.

If you are in a *lucky* Personal *Year* to gamble (number 5, 8, 3, 2, 9 or 7), try to *also* pick a *lucky* Personal *Month* (number 5, 8, 3, 2, 9 or 7) *and* a lucky Personal *Day* (number 5, 8, 3, 2, 9 or 7) on which to gamble. Try to *avoid* the *unlucky* Months and Days (numbers 1, 4, and 6), if possible.

> *Note:* Your best chance to win is when you choose your lucky Personal Year, Month and Day AND COMBINE them with your Astrological Sun Sign dates (refer to Chapter Four).

CHAPTER FOUR
GAMBLING AND ASTROLOGY

Your Astrological Sun Sign is based upon your birthday. Your chances to win are enhanced when the daily Sun (in the sky) is in a sign *favorable* to YOUR Sun Sign. Some dates are better than others; therefore, I will list them as great (the first best) and good (the second best). Locate your Sun Sign in the following list. Listed under your Sun Sign are the *FAVORABLE DATES TO GAMBLE ACCORDING TO YOUR SUN SIGN.*

ARIES (those born March 21-April 19)
January 20-February 18 (good)
May 21-June 20 (good)
July 23-August 22 (great)
November 22-December 21 (great)

TAURUS (those born April 20-May 20)
January 1-10 (great)
February 19-March 20 (good)
June 21-July 22 (good)
August 23-September 22 (great)
December 22-31 (great)

GEMINI (those born May 21-June 20)
January 20-February 18 (great)
March 21-April 19 (good)
July 23-August 22 (good)
September 23-October 22 (great)

CANCER (those born June 21-July 22)
February 19-March 20 (great)
April 20-May 20 (good)
August 23-September 22 (good)
October 23-November 21 (great)

LEO (those born July 23-August 22)
March 21-April 19 (great)
May 21-June 20 (good)
September 23-October 22 (good)
November 22-December 21 (great)
VIRGO (those born August 23-September 22)
January 1-19 (great)
April 20-May 20 (great)
June 21-July 22 (good)
October 23-November 21 (good)
December 22-31 (great)
LIBRA (those born September 23-October 22)
January 20-February 18 (great)
May 21-June 20 (great)
July 23-August 22 (good)
November 22-December 21 (good)
SCORPIO (those born October 23-November 21)
January 1-19 (good)
February 19-March 20 (great)
June 21-July 22 (great)
August 23-September 22 (good)
SAGITTARIUS (those born November 22-December 21)
January 20-February 18 (good)
March 21-April 19 (great)
July 23-August 22 (great)
September 23-October 22 (good)
CAPRICORN (those born December 22-January 19)
February 19-March 20 (good)
April 20-May 20 (great)
August 23-September 22 (great)
October 23-November 21 (good)

AQUARIUS (those born January 20-February 18)
March 21-April 19 (good)
May 21-June 20 (great)
September 23-October 22 (great)
November 22-December 21 (good)
PISCES (those born February 19-March 20)
January 1-19 (good)
April 20-May 20 (good)
June 21-July 22 (great)
October 23-November 21 (great)

CHOOSING COMPATIBLE ASTROLOGICAL
SIGN NUMBERS FOR GAMBLING

You have heard the expressions, "Oh, our signs are compatible." Or, "We are *not* compatible." Thus, some couples are not compatible because their Astrological Sun Signs are inharmonious to each other. Other people are compatible because their Sun Signs *are* harmonious to each other.

Numbers have the same affinity as Sun Sign Astrology does to people in a relationship. The planets are in various signs of the Zodiac every day. These planets, and the signs they are in, correspond to different numbers and their rays affect us here on Earth. Therefore, it is logical that the numbers to which the signs and planets correspond to can have an effect on everything we do, just as the signs and planets affect us. Because certain signs are compatible with each other (thus making for a great relationship), you can also use their compatible (and corresponding) numbers for gambling.

Find your Sun Sign below (dates are given for Sun Signs, if you don't know yours) on the preceding pages. When you bet or play with numbers, use these numbers for gambling.

For Example: Your Sun Sign is Aries (number 13). Thus, you would play number 13. Because Aries (number 13) is compatible with Leo (number 19), you could also play number 19 or any of the remaining numbers. If you are playing Three Digit Numbers, you could pick number 7 (Sagittarius) and number 14 (Taurus), which equals 714 (when added together as a Three digit number). Or with a four-digit number, combine 13 (Aries) with 19 (Leo). When adding them together as a four-digit number, it equal 1319.

Note: You do not have to break these numbers down.

COMPATIBLE SIGNS
If you are an ARIES

Number 13 (corresponds to Aries) is most compatible with Number 19 (Leo) or 7 (Sagittarius). Next in harmony is 17 (Gemini) or 9 (Aquarius). Last in harmony is 14 (Taurus), or 12 (Pisces).

If you are a TAURUS

Number 14 (corresponds to Taurus) is most compatible with 2 (Virgo) or 8 (Capricorn). Next in harmony is 18 (Cancer) or 12 (Pisces). Last in harmony is 13 (Aries) or 17 (Gemini).

If you are a GEMINI

Number 17 (corresponds to Gemini) is most compatible with 3 (Libra) or 9 (Aquarius). Next in harmony is 19 (Leo) or 13 (Aries). Last in harmony is 14 (Taurus) or 18 (Cancer).

If you are a CANCER

Number 18 (corresponds to Cancer) is most compatible with 4 (Scorpio) or 12 (Pisces). Next in harmony is 2 (Virgo) or 14 (Taurus). Last in harmony is 17 (Gemini) or 19 (Leo).

If you are a LEO

Number 19 (corresponds to Leo) is most compatible with 1: (Aries) or 7 (Sagittarius). Next in harmony is 3 (Libra) or 1 (Gemini). Last in harmony is 18 (Cancer) or 2 (Virgo).

If you are a VIRGO

Number 2 (corresponds to Virgo) is most compatible with 8 (Capricorn) or 14 (Taurus). Next in harmony is 4 (Scorpio) or 18 (Cancer). Last in harmony is 19 (Leo) or 3 (Libra).

If you are a LIBRA

Number 3 (corresponds to Libra) is most compatible with 9 (Aquarius) or 17 (Gemini). Next in harmony is 7 (Sagittarius) or 19 (Leo). Last in harmony is 2 (Virgo) or 4 (Scorpio).

If you are a SCORPIO

Number 4 (corresponds to Scorpio) is most compatible with 12 (Pisces) or 18 (Cancer). Next in harmony is 2 (Virgo) or 8 (Capricorn). Last in harmony is 3 (Libra) or 7 (Sagittarius).

If you are a SAGITTARIUS

Number 7 (corresponds to Sagittarius) is most compatible with 13 (Aries) or 19 (Leo). Next in harmony is 3 (Libra) or 9 (Aquarius). Last in harmony is 4 (Scorpio) or 8 (Capricorn).

If you are a CAPRICORN

Number 8 (corresponds to Capricorn) is most compatible with 2 (Virgo) or 14 (Taurus). Next in harmony is 4 (Scorpio) or 12 (Pisces). Last in harmony is 7 (Sagittarius) or 9 (Aquarius).

If you are an AQUARIUS

Number 9 (corresponds to Aquarius) is most compatible with 3 (Libra) or 17 (Gemini). Next in harmony is 7 (Sagittarius) or 13 (Aries). Last in harmony is 8 (Capricorn) or 12 (Pisces).

If you are a PISCES

Number 12 (corresponds to Pisces) is most compatible with 4 (Scorpio) or 18 (Cancer). Next in harmony is 8 (Capricorn) or 14 (Taurus). Last in harmony is 9 (Aquarius) or 13 (Aries).

Note: The preceding are SUN SIGN numbers. You will notice that there are missing numbers: 1, 5, 6, 10, 11, 15, 16, 20, 21 and 22. (These numbers correspond to PLANETS). To discover if ANY NUMBER *is* LUCKY FOR YOU, you need to have your ASTRODYNES calculated by a computer service which can provide you with this information. I use:

Astro Numeric Service
P. O. Box 336
Ashland, OR 97520
Toll-free number: 1-800-MAPPING

Astro Numeric Service charges a small fee ($2.50 plus a handling charge of $2.00 - prices subject to change). You must give your day, month, year, place and time of birth to them and ask for THE HERMETIC SYSTEM OF ASTRODYNES. You will receive a computer printout page similar to the example on page 6 of *Gloria Swanson.* Instructions follow.

ASTRODYNES

The use of ASTRODYNES IS THE ONLY ACCURATE METHOD in Astrology *for finding* YOUR LUCKY NUMBERS. It is based upon the harmonious signs and planets in your own individualized horoscope - your day, month, year, place and time of birth. The mathematics of calculating the Astrodynes is very complicated, tedious and time-consuming. The computer printout you receive from the computer service is the document you need in order to discover what your lucky numbers are.

How to Read Your Astrodyne Computer Printout

The example of a computer printout on page 6 is that of the legendary movie star *Gloria Swanson*. It is easy to read-here's how! Practice on this example before doing your own.

THE BEST PLANETS

Look at the computer printout page of *Gloria Swanson's* horoscope on page 6. The top left column is headed by PLANETS. The "Harmony" column is the one you need to look at; therefore, I have marked with an "X" all the other columns. Thus, the mistake of getting in a wrong column is avoided. Do the same, when you receive your Astrodyne computer printout page in the mail.

Take the HIGHEST FIGURE (in the "Harmony" Column) WITHOUT A MINUS SYMBOL. (Don't let the "Harmony" column fool you, because those minus figures underneath it represent discord, not harmony!). *The first best planet is the one with the highest figure without a minus symbol.* For instance, on *Gloria Swanson's* Astrodyne page, the highest figure without a minus symbol is 31.81. To the left of that figure in the first column under PLANETS is Venus, which means that Venus is the BEST PLANET in *Gloria Swanson's* horoscope. Her second best planet is Jupiter with the second highest figure, 11.02. The third best planet is Mercury with the third highest figure, 5.19. Her fourth best planet is the MC (not a planet, so disregard both it and the ASC) at 2.24. *(Note:* The MC and ASC are angles and are not taken into consideration when figuring your best planets). The

38

fifth best planet is Pluto at 2.01, and the sixth best planet is Uranus at 2.39.

THE BEST SIGNS

Look at the computer printout page of *Gloria Swanson's* horoscope on page 6. Look in the middle of the page - middle section - and you will see a column headed, "SIGNS". To the right of it are columns "Power", "%", and "Harmony". The "Harmony" column is the only one you need to look at; therefore, I have marked with an "X" all the other columns. Thus, the mistake of getting in the wrong column is avoided. Do the same when you receive your computer printout Astrodyne page in the mail.

Take the HIGHEST FIGURE (in the "Harmony" column_ WITHOUT A MINUS SYMBOL. (Don't let the "Harmony" column fool you, because those minus figures underneath it represent discord, not harmony). *The first best sign is the one with the highest figure without a minus symbol*. For instance, on *Gloria Swanson's* Astrodyne page, the highest figure without a minus symbol is 28.43. To the left of that figure under the column headed "SIGNS" is Aquarius, which means that Aquarius is the best sign in the horoscope of *Gloria Swanson*. Her second best sign is Taurus which has the second highest figure, 15.90. The third best sign is Libra with the third highest figure, 12.06. Her fourth best sign is Scorpio at 7.00, and her fifth best sign is Virgo at 2.59.

CONVERTING SIGNS AND PLANETS
TO YOUR LUCKY NUMBERS

To convert your best signs and planets to numbers, merely look them up in the Table on page 40. An example of *Gloria*

Swanson's best signs and planets converted to Lucky Numbers follows:

GLORIA SWANSON

Best Planets		Lucky Numbers	Best Signs		Lucky Numbers
Venus	=	6	Aquarius	=	9
Jupiter	=	5	Taurus	=	14
Mercury	=	1	Libra	=	3
Pluto	=	22	Scorpio	=	4
Uranus	=	10	Virgo	=	2

Table: Astrological Correspondence To Numbers

1 = Mercury		8 = Capricorn		15 = Saturn	
2 = Virgo		9 = Aquarius		16 = Mars	
3 = Libra		10 = Uranus		17 = Gemini	
4 = Scorpio		11 = Neptune		18 = Cancer	
5 = Jupiter		12 = Pisces		19 = Leo	
6 = Venus		13 = Aries		20 = Moon	
7 = Sagittarius		14 = Taurus		21 = Sun	
				22 = Pluto	

What if there are *not any* lucky numbers on your Astrodyne printout page? It is possible for this to happen. I knew someone who was in this position and she followed my advice and did very well with all the various forms of gambling in which she partook. She used the number (on her Astrodyne printout page) that had the smallest figure with a minus in front of it. In other words, she had Neptune listed with -0.02 and it corresponds to number 11, which she played when she gambled.

The figure listed on the computer page with the highest minus figure is the worst sign and/or planet in the horoscope. Therefore, when all of the signs and planets are listed with a minus figure, select the one with the lowest figure. Then look on the TABLE: Astrological correspondences to Numbers, and convert the sign and/or planet to its corresponding number.

Of course, it is risky playing with numbers that are not the luckiest for you, but perhaps you will select a lucky *day* to gamble (pages 18-28) that may bring you good fortune.

You may wonder, where did the system of Numbers vibrating to Signs and Planets originate? It is based upon the Hermetic system, as set forth in C. C. Zalin's book *The Secret Tarot*, published by *The Church of Light*. In ancient Egypt, where the Temple of Luxor was built (and still stands) as a temple to the Sun-God *Amon*, was a select group called *The Brotherhood of Luxor*. These people followed certain principles and used a particular system called *Hermetic*. This system included spiritual areas, astrology, numerology, alchemy and magic. Only a chosen few knew the secrets it contained.

During the Dark Ages, the doctrines involving the *Hermetic* system were kept hidden in various forms of secret seals and symbols. Therefore, this Table (on page 40) is the same which the ancients used and is quite unrelated to other systems of numerology. This system uses astrology and contains the same original numbers used throughout the ages.

In this *Hermetic* system of numbers that vibrate to signs and planets, there are 22 numbers used. The 12 signs and 10 planets each govern particular types of actions, thoughts and behaviors. A specific number vibrates to each sign or planet. Thus, every time these numbers are used, certain forces are set in motion, which explains why some numbers are lucky for you and others are not. If a sign or planet is harmonious for you, good luck is then attracted when you utilize the numbers corresponding to them. Thus, from the foregoing, you can see how important it is to have a number that will be lucky for you.

GAMBLING WITH YOUR LUCKY NUMBERS

Your lucky numbers may be used in all forms of gambling where numbers are used. When playing roulette, you may pick the numbers that are lucky for you, and you may want to continue with these same numbers throughout the game. When you go to the race track, regardless of whether it is horses or greyhound dogs that you are betting on, the procedures are the same. At the track, you may want to pick a race number that is lucky for you, i.e., 7 as in the 7th race. Also in the same race, you may want to select a post position number that is lucky for you or the number on the horse or the greyhound. You may want to use your best lucky number on the race, post position, or horse or greyhound with that number. Or you may want to spread around all of your lucky numbers, i.e., one lucky number on a horse, the other on the post position and another one on the race number.

You may want to select numbers that are lucky for you when using the point spreads in football, baseball or with a prize fight. For instance, in a prize fight, round 8 could be auspicious for you because 8 happens to be one of your propitious numbers. In football, since there are four quarters, select the quarter that is lucky for you, if you wish. For example: If number 1 is a lucky number for you, use the point spreads in that quarter. Or if number 4 is lucky, use that quarter for the point spread. Also pick the point-spread numbers that are your best. Baseball has nine innings; therefore, you may want to pick the inning number that is lucky for you and make your bet according to the score that corresponds to your lucky numbers. This principle applies to all sports - tennis, basketball, ice hockey, and so on.

If it is lotto or the lottery you are playing and you have more than one lucky number, you may play all, or part, of them. You may also switch the numbers around. For instance, in the *Hermetic* system of numbers (as given on the Table on page 40), you will notice that none of the numbers are more than 22. If a number breaks down to a number from 1 to 22, then you may use that number too. For instance, if number 6 is lucky for you, you may also use numbers 24, 33, 42, 51, 60, 105, 123, 132, 141, 150, 204, 213, 222, 231, 240, 303, 312, 321, 330, 402, 411, 420, 501, 510, and 600. All of the preceding numbers, when added, break down to the number 6. Therefore, apply this same principle with one, or all, of your lucky numbers. Do not add zero; omit it.

When purchasing raffle tickets, add the numbers beforehand, if possible. If you receive sweepstakes numbers in the mail, add them, and, if they are lucky for you, your chances to win are enhanced. Remember - *any number* MORE THAN 22 MUST be broken down to a number from 1 to 22.

COMBINING LUCKY DAYS AND NUMBERS

In Chapter One, you are shown how to find your LUCKY DAYS according to numerology. In this Chapter (Four), you are shown how to find your LUCKY NUMBERS according to astrology. Now what you need to do is correlate them so they work together in your favor.

As mentioned previously, on page 28, the luckiest personal numerology years, months or days on which to gamble are numbers 2, 3, 5, 8 and 9. If you are not in one of these years, months or days, you are taking a risk and could lose plenty. Then, once you know you are in a Year Month or Day during which is

43

lucky for you to gamble, select a date when you are in a lucky year to gamble, a month that is fortunate to gamble and a day that is lucky to gamble. For example: You are in a 5 year ... select a month - 8 - that means that March of that year is an eighth month ... and you can select a day in March that is favorable, such as March 6th. (a five day for you).

Buy your lotto or lottery ticket on one of your lucky days (and also make sure you are in a lucky month and year), and check to see that the drawing of the lottery numbers is also on one of these same days. Use your lucky numbers also on one of these same days. When you buy raffle or sweepstakes tickets, add the numbers beforehand, if possible, and be sure that the numbers on them are lucky for you. Also, purchase tickets on your lucky days If there are many numbers already selected on a ticket, add them and take the sum total and break it down to a number from 1 to 22. and, if it is one of your lucky numbers, your chances to win are enhanced. Also look for the date the sweepstakes winner is to be announced; see if it correlates with your lucky year, month and day. If it does, your chance to be a winner is improved.

Example:

You may want to buy a lotto ticket that has 6 sets of numbers. Your lucky numbers are 5 and 6. You can use numbers that are more than 22, but they must add up to 5 or 6. For instance, 23, 32, and 41 add up to 5. And 24, 33, and 42 add up to 6. Therefore, when playing the lotto (or lottery), you may use any of these numbers in any combination desired and you'll be using your lucky numbers. Also, make sure that you gamble on your Lucky days according to numerology, pages 28.

Example:

If you are playing the lottery 3-digit numbers, then you may want to use your lucky numbers as follows: Your lucky number is 7

Select 3-digit numbers that, when added up, will break down to 7. If you pick 232, 331 or 421, add them separately and break that down to a single-digit figured, and they will all equal your lucky number - 7! Also make sure that you gamble on your lucky days according to numerology, pages 28.

Example:

If you are playing the lottery 4-digit numbers, then you may want to use your lucky numbers as follows: your lucky number is 14. Select 4-digit numbers that, when added together, will break down to 14. If you pick 1580, 2471 or 3551, add them separately and they break down to 14. Also, make sure that you gamble on your lucky days according to numerology, pages 28.

Example:

If number 6 is your lucky number, make an important decision on that day only if it is *also* favorable for you according to the day you are in when using numerology. Do not make *decisions* if you are in a Personal Day number 2, 4 or 9.

Example:

If numbers 5 and 7 are lucky numbers for you, ask for a raise on either the 5th., 7th., 23rd. (it adds up to 5) or 25th. (it adds up to 7) of the month. However, check that one of these dates is *also* a favorable Personal Day number, according to the day you are in when using numerology. Do not ask for a raise if you are in a Personal Day number 2, 4 or 9.

Example:

Socialize on a number 1, 3, 5 or 8 day according to Personal numerology; however, if these days happen to fall on the 3rd., 6th. or 14th. day of the month (good days to socialize), so much the better - you will have a grand time! Do not socialize on the 8th. and 15th. of the month (days when you tend to be serious).

However, if a personal numerology day is 3, 5 or 8, it may counteract the discordant day (18th. or 15th. of the month).

Example:

Borrow money on a favorable day according to your personal numerology day *and borrow* in the *amount (sums)* of your lucky number. For instance, if January 14th is a 6 day for you according to your personal day numerology. Your lucky number, according to ASTRODYNES, is 7. Borrow either $700, $1,006, $1,052, $2,500, $3,200, and so on. All of these lucky numbers break down to a 7. If the number 14 is *also* a lucky number for you, then the 14th. of the month is a favorable time to do it. Also make sure that you are in a favorable Month and Year according to personal numerology. If you are in a 5 year for January and the month of January is a 6 month for you, then this could be a super time to borrow money - according to personal numerology.

Example:

Use your lucky number for the day of the month to plan an important event. Perhaps you want to give a party. Plan it for a date that is lucky for you. For instance, say your lucky number, according to ASTRODYNES is 5; therefore, on December 5th. give a party. If you want to double-check this date to make sure that it is a superb day - use your personal numerology day also. If it happens to be a 3 or 5 day (according to personal numerology) you will have a wonderful time!

Example:

When ordering ads to be printed (or other items to be made) order in quantities that total your lucky number, according to ASTRODYNES. For instance, 5 is lucky for you - so order 500 ads (flyers). You will find the work performed and the service better than at other times. Also, combine this with your personal day number - do it when you are either a number 1, 3, 4, or 6 day.

CHAPTER FIVE
VARIOUS USES OF LUCKY NUMBERS

To attract success and good fortune, it's important that you use your lucky numbers as much as possible and in as many areas as you can.

Your Telephone Number

According to C. C. Zain *in* his book *Imponderable Forces* (published by *The Church of Light,* "... when an individual is called by telephone many times per day, those calling him think of him while calling the number ... and if the person is called over the telephone frequently, this vibratory rate, so often projected by thought to him, has considerable influence." How it will affect him depends upon the harmony or discord in his horoscope as indicated by ASTRODYNES.

If you are thinking about starting a business, be sure and get a telephone number that is lucky for you. Often, you are given a choice, and now there are names that your telephone can have instead of just numbers. If it is a number you are using, again, select a number that vibrates to your lucky number. If it is a name instead of a number, or a combination of numbers and a name, add the letters (see Table - Letter Correspondences to Numbers, page 49), so you can convert these letters to a lucky number. Further along, I will explain how to convert letters to numbers (page 49).

If you are already in business and the telephone number you have is unlucky for you, it may be expensive to change it, but could well be worth the expense. If you wonder, "Why is business so slow?" Perhaps the telephone does not ring as much as you would like because the number vibrates to an unlucky number. It is possible that the public just does not tune in to this number. If you paid extra money for new cards and stationery, with a new and lucky phone number printed on them it is most likely that your telephone would be ringing all of the time - all because you have a lucky phone number.

If you are a female and wonder why you do not have many dates, perhaps it is because your telephone number is unlucky. Perhaps it vibrates to number 8 or 15 - numbers that correspond to business rather than love. Therefore, if numbers 3, 6, or 14 are lucky for your, change your telephone number to one of them (the final digits of your telephone number will be broken down to a 3, 6 or 14) and wait for romance to enter your life. It may not be such a long wait!

For local calls, the area code is not important. However, if you meet someone on a trip who lives in another state or country, then that individual will think of you in relation to your total number *including* the area code. But THE STRONGEST THOUGHT will be more with your number than the area code and number. If you want further contact with this person, it is best to have the area code and number as both lucky numbers; however, don't worry about that because it's not that important. Perhaps the two of you are compatible astrologically, or your area code and number are lucky for him/her!

Table: Letter Correspondences to Numbers

A	= 1	H	= 8	O	= 16	TS	= 18
B	= 2	I	= 10	P	= 17	TZ	= 18
C	= 11	J	= 10	Q	= 19	U	= 6
CH	= 8	K	= 11	R	= 20	V	= 6
D	= 4	L	= 12	S	= 21	W	= 6
E	= 5	M	= 13	SH	= 18	X	= 15
F	= 17	N	= 14	T	= 22	Y	= 10
G	= 3			TH	= 9	Z	= 7

Adding Telephone Numbers and Letters

If your telephone number is 325-4126, add 3 + 2 + 5 + 4 + 1 + 2 + 6, and it equals 23. (This is more than 22; therefore, break it down to a smaller number from 1 to 22). 23 breaks down to 5. If your area code is 215, add that to the 23 (2 + 1 + 5 and add the 8 + 23 = 31), break it down (3 + 1 + 4), which is the vibratory number for the telephone 215-325-4126.

To Add Letters

If you request a telephone number *and* name, such as 222-ROSE, add it as follows; 2 + 2 + 2 + 20 (for the R - refer to the above Table) + 16 (for the O) + 21 (for the S) + 5 (for the E), and it equals 68. Then break it down to a smaller number from 1 to 22 (68 is more than 22; therefore, it needs to be broken down) and 6 + 8 = 14, a number that, hopefully, is lucky for you!

Your Automobile License Plate

Are you aware that if your automobile number vibrates to either number 10 or 16, *AND* IS UNLUCKY FOR YOU, that you may be more inclined to attract an accident because these numbers are involved in catastrophes of this nature *when unlucky* for an individual? If your license plate vibrates to number 16, and you cannot change it immediately, wear green - or perhaps your car is

49

green - in either case, this helps counteract discord. If your license plate vibrates to number 10 and you cannot change it immediately, wear purple - or perhaps your car is purple - in either case, this helps counteract discord. DO NOT *wear red or have a red car* because red enhances the number 16 discordant vibration - that is, *if it is unlucky for you.*

In many cities, it is popular to have your name on a license plate. Again, choose a name that is lucky for you by adding it in the same way as explained under the preceding category *Adding Telephone Numbers* and Letter, page 49. The name should vibrate to your lucky number.

If you must choose between a name or numbers on your license plate, keep in mind that numbers are not as powerful as names. People see numbers on a license plate and it is not as effective, or as easy to remember, as a name. It is best to have your license plate vibrate to something that is lucky for you, regardless of whether you use a name or numbers on your license plate.

Seat Numbers

Have you ever gone to a show and squirmed in your seat? Was it difficult to sit still at the opera - especially when you were enthralled with the music and singing? Or did you fall asleep at the theatre? Or perhaps the person next to you was annoying because he/she was indulging in chit-chat throughout the ballet? Or did you dislike the concert? Did you have a miserable time at the ball game because a stranger spilled a soft drink on your lap? Did you ever fly in an airplane with a passenger who kept kicking the back of your seat? Are you aware that these circumstances could have been prevented had you been sitting in a seat that vibrated to your lucky number?

The next time you take a *jet*, pick a seat number that is lucky for you, and perhaps the flight will be the smoothest one you've ever experienced. This can be very beneficial and mind-relieving if you are afraid to fly. The fear may be eased because you know that you are sitting in a seat that's lucky for you. If you arrived too late to choose your lucky seat, try to select a number that vibrates to 5. The number vibrates to Jupiter, the luckiest planet in astrology; it represents divine protection and confidence, and is a fortunate influence. If there are not any numbers that add up to your lucky numbers, or to 5, look on YOUR Astrodyne computer printout page and choose the number that gives the lowest minus figure in either the *Signs* or *Planets* section.

You will enjoy the *ballet, concert, opera or theatre, lecture, movie or trade show* more if you purchase tickets that vibrate to your lucky numbers. But what about the person who accompanies you? Do you know his or her lucky numbers? Or what if someone else buys the tickets and you are a guest? You could also ask to look at the tickets, add their numbers quickly and sit in the seat that is the least discordant (the sign or planet that has the smallest minus figure) according to your Astrodynes on the computer printout page ... that is, if none of the seat numbers is lucky for you. Of course, you may have to explain to your host why you want a particular seat. However, if you are the one who is buying the tickets and you do not know your companion's lucky numbers, purchase tickets that add up to either number 3, 5, 6, or 7. These numbers correspond to the luckiest signs and planets in astrology and thus enhance your enjoyment of the entertainment.

If you purchase tickets for the *circus, ice show, aquacade* or any other *extravaganza-type* show, then select seats which vibrate to 11 or 12. If either one is lucky for you, the corresponding sign or planet may influence you to escape to the world of fantasy, thus

51

satisfying your every fancy and love of glamour. If either one of these numbers is unlucky for you, you may be disappointed, fall asleep and be up in the clouds in your own daydream world and not even be aware that a show is in progress.

If you attend a *lecture* or some type of *show* that *exercises your mind*, pick a seat number that adds up to either 1, 2, or 17 - that is, if one of them is lucky for you. Otherwise, you may squirm, fidget and be disturbed by the loud chatter or whispers of those seated nearby, especially if you're the nervous and restless type. Or, if you are sitting in a number 2 seat, you may be so critical of the show, or its performers, that not one moment is enjoyed.

If you attend the serious type of *lecture, show, recital or concert*, pick seat numbers that add up to 2, 4, 8 or 15 - that is, if they are lucky for you. Otherwise, you may gripe, complain criticize, cry and be miserable - especially if you were born with these same characteristics.

Use your lucky numbers to pick a seat number for *sporting events*, such as football, baseball, basketball, jai-alai, ice hockey the fights, the *Olympics* or the races (horse, harness, greyhound). If you like to yell, scream and root for a team or a person, pick a seat number that vibrates to 13 or 16. If these numbers are lucky for you, you'll be loaded with energy and your voice will be louder and stronger than usual. However, the same may apply if these numbers are *unlucky* for you. But the difference, in this case, is you may argue, throw a temperamental scene or get involved in a fight that leads to a brawl - especially if these traits are part of your behavioral pattern. If the numbers 13 or 16 *are lucky* for you, you'll be in good spirits - especially if your favorite team wins.

If either number 1 or 17 is unlucky for you and you sit in a seat that vibrates to one of these numbers, you may be confused, have itchy feet and get up and down so much that you end up pacing the floor. These actions are enhanced if they are part of your nature. If these seat numbers are lucky for you, then your nerves are, probably, in good shape and you are less inclined to drive others berserk with your behavior!

If you are not in the mood for a good cry, stay away from seat numbers that add up to 8, 11, 15, 18 and 20 - especially if you are attending a funeral or a tragic or sentimental play or movie. These seat numbers correspond to signs and planets whose traits represent emotion and sensitivity. If this is your normal nature, it will be enhanced more just by sitting in one of the seats with any of those numbers.

You will feel important if you sit in a seat that adds up to either 19 or 21, especially if royalty, politicians or celebrities are in the audience. However, if either one of these numbers is unlucky for you and you are in a seat that vibrates to one of them, you must guard against your ego getting deflated because you were snubbed by a VIP.

If you enjoy the crowds or want to feel spiritually uplifted, pick a seat that vibrates to number 11, if it is lucky for you. If it is unlucky for you, possibly you'll fear the crowd, attract theft or prefer to hibernate.

If you're the type who is nervous, restless, talkative, fidgety, easily bored or dislikes confinement, don't select a seat number that adds up to 1, 2, 7, 9, 10, 13, 16, 17, 18 or 20. These numbers enhance these traits. If this applies to you, sit in a seat number that adds up to 4, 8, 14, 15 or 19 because you'll be inclined to keep quiet, concentrate and sit glued to your seat like an immovable object.

If you tend to gripe, complain or criticize, avoid sitting in a seat that adds up to 2, 4, 8 and 15 because these numbers enhance these traits. Try to sit in a seat number that adds up to 3, 5, 6 or 7 because in these vibrations you tend to be easy-going, in high fun-loving spirits and make the best of your surroundings.

If you tend to be impatient or temperamental, avoid seat numbers that add up to 13 and 16 because these traits are enhanced with these number vibrations. Try to sit in seat numbers that add up to 3, 6, 11, 12 or 14 because you'll be inclined to relax, take it easy and curb emotional upsets.

If you tend to be unpredictable and leave a lecture, show or sporting event before it is finished, avoid sitting in a seat number that adds up to 1, 9, 10 or 17. These numbers bring out those traits more and you may be too jumpy and erratic. Try to sit in a seat that adds up to 4, 8, 14, 15, 19 or 21 because in these seat-number vibrations you are likely to stay in your seat and see the entire show.

If you tend to be emotional, sensitive and cry easily, avoid sitting in seat numbers that add up to 12, 18 or 20 because you'll tend to over-react in these seat-number vibrations. To be calm, cool, collected and unemotional, sit in seat numbers 2, 4, 5, 7, 9, 10, 13, 14 17, 19, 21 or 22.

If you tend to be fun-loving, laugh a lot, and are happy-go-lucky, you'll really enjoy yourself in a seat number that adds up to a 5 or 7 because these traits are enhanced in these seat-number vibrations ... even if they are unlucky for you.

If you want to relax in a seat and take pleasure in the entertainment, select a seat number that adds up to 3, 6 or 14. Enjoy yourself - that is, if these numbers are lucky for you.

ADDRESSES - BOX, HOME, OFFICE

C. C. Zain, in his book *Imponderable Forces* (published by *The Church of Light),* states that a number of a room in an office, building where you work or post office box "...usually stands out in the mind apart from the name of the street, building or post office." He believes that "...the number is the important element of such an address." He also goes on to say, "And when many people think of this number each day in association with the person using it, that person receives quite a bombardment of thoughts of the particular vibratory key of the number. Also, he becomes accustomed to think of himself as associated with this number. And in this case, the number has quite an appreciable effect on him." Of course, how this number will affect you is dependent upon the harmony and discord of the signs and planets in your horoscope, as measured by *Astrodynes.*

ADDING NUMBERS AND LETTERS

Add the numbers of the building where you live or work *and* your suite, apartment or post office box number. Use the Tables on pages 40 and 49. Keep in mind that numbers, when added together, cannot be more than 22; if they are, break them down to a final number from 1 to 22. Omit zeros. To add letters, take the letter and add its corresponding number to any other numbers. For instance, your apartment number is 4B ... B = 2; therefore, add it to the 4 and your answer is 6, which is the vibratory number for apartment 4B - Venus. If Venus is listed on your Astrodyne computer printout page under PLANETS with numbers that do NOT have a minus, then your apartment number 4B is lucky for you. However, if a minus symbol is given, then it is NOT a harmonious vibration for you.

All sorts of incidents occur when you live in a place which is not lucky for you. A client of mine was murdered in an apartment which had a number that was unlucky for her. For years, she tried to listen to my advice to move but obstacles prevented here. A number 8 and also number 15 are the most difficult apartment numbers for people to move from. 8 is represented by the stubborn Capricorn goat that doesn't budge and 15 is represented by the planet Saturn which likes to stay put and causes delays in making changes. A friend of mine had financial reversals in a number 15 apartment which was unlucky for him; he ended up living off welfare. If an 8 or 15 is lucky for you, you need not fear unhappy or poverty conditions.

An unlucky number vibration can hold you back from business and romantic success. Thus, it's important to live in a place that in conducive to happiness and which brings material rewards. A client of mine was very lucky to attract great wealth in a number 14 apartment and office vibration and a number 5 building. When she moved from that office/apartment, her luck wasn't as good. The number 14 was her luckiest zodiac sign-number according to *Astrodynes*. When she moved, she changed her vibrations to numbers that were not lucky - but she liked the new place and took her chances. Later, she regretted her decision. Her love life and pocketbook suffered until she was able to relocate.

I have knows people who lived in apartments that added up to numbers 9 and 10. These numbers, when unlucky for an individual, bring shocks, surprises, upheavals and make the person living there very abrupt and erratic. The unexpected occurrences in one case was that of a guest who tried to commit suicide by slashing her wrists. Furthermore, the apartment was like Grand Central Station, with a constant flow of people - clients, guests, friends or relatives visiting. Another guest had a heart attack, but lived through it. A computer broke down daily. Electrical appliances were always in need of repair. Fuses went out in one room.

Fights took place. A guest had two friends over who turned out to be a pimp and a prostitute. A reformed alcoholic went back to heavy drinking and lost his business. Another person went bankrupt. So, all of the stories I have heard from the people who lived in a 9 or 10 number environment have been interesting and mind-boggling! Of course, all of these individuals didn't stay long in their apartments - leases were broken and moves were sudden ... but remedied the unlucky situations.

If your apartment number is unlucky for you, perhaps the floor it is on is a lucky number. For instance, your apartment number vibrates to 15 and your floor is 5; the number 15 vibrates to Saturn, the *worst* planet in astrology, and 5 vibrates to Jupiter, the *luckiest* planet in astrology - thus, they tend to cancel each other out and the Jupiter vibration helps a little. It is possible that, under the Jupiter influence, for the floor vibration, that all your neighbors on that floor are extremely helpful and friendly. This is especially true if Jupiter, number 5, is lucky in your horoscope, which would be indicated on the ASTRODYNE computer printout page.

Numbers can be applied in relation to a house, room, suite, office, floor, building and an apartment. If you work in a *harmonious place*, it is easier to get lucky breaks such as pay raises and promotions. If you are in business for yourself, you may expand due to an increase in profits. However, if you are in an office or a building that is an *unlucky* number for you, it is possible that you will have difficulty with co-workers, be held back from advancing to a higher position, or find yourself griping because you are not receiving the salary you think you deserve.

This type of environment could affect your health and make you miserable to the point of alienating your loved ones. Thus, you can see how important it is to live in a place that will bring you happiness, prosperity and good health.

To discover how a *number may affect you*, read the pages that follow. The text applies to people in varying degrees and is dependent upon the dominant elements in an individual horoscope. In other words, this is a stereotype of the numbers, signs and planets and is dependent upon how strong a number, sign and planet is in your horoscope as to how much it fits your situation.

A NUMBER 1 (MERCURY) OR NUMBER 17 (GEMINI) ENVIRONMENT

If Lucky For You: You are in and out of the home. The decor is constantly changed. Books and papers are topsy-turvy and can be found just about everywhere. Bookcases are filled without a space between the books. Lots of chatter fills the air. The telephones never stop ringing and several conversations may be going on simultaneously. Neighbors come and leave quickly. The house or apartment seems like *Grand Central Station* because it is overcrowded when friends, relatives, associates, neighbors and acquaintances drop by unexpectedly. There is lots of hustle-bustle in this atmosphere. Intellectual conversations are heard. Knowledge is exchanged. Continual excitement reigns. Everybody is busy doing a chore or talking - gossip reigns supreme. The cooking and cleaning are done in a flash. Hands move so fast, others can barely see them move.

The office is a hub of constant activity with the telephone constantly ringing, and lots of noise as everyone talks at the same time. There is not a dull moment or lag during the entire time pent there. Action is taken quickly. Projects are initiated at the drop of a hat and finished in practically no time. Ideas are born that may make the profits roll in; in fact, there is never an end to the brainstorms that occur in this environment. All views are expressed with intelligence and are brilliantly executed.

Unlucky For You: The sound of the chatter and idle gossip is overpowering. There do not seem to be any secrets that are kept or held sacred. Projects are tackled so hurriedly that mistakes are made easily. Constant indecisiveness causes big blunders that are costly. There is a lack of continuity in business deals. Work is left undone. It is difficult to finish a task. This is a noisy environment; the telephone rings constantly, people dash about in various directions and the talking doesn't seem to cease. It is difficult to concentrate on the daily tasks. There are too many risks taken in business that attract continual losses. You may fidget, have the jitters and swear you are on the verge of a nervous breakdown.

At home, you are a nervous wreck - things are spilled, broken, knocked over and projects left unfinished. Perhaps one wall is painted and the other left undone for several months. Clothes are left strung all over the place. Food is left on the countertops, and dishes are left in the sink. Blouses or shirts are thrown in the closet on top of other clothes as you frantically try to tidy up before guests arrive. The decor is changed constantly and mixed with objects that do not match. Others may become dizzy from the various colors and abstract designs on the drapes, couch and chairs. You may not be home much, and when you are it looks as if a tornado hit the place!

A NUMBER 2 (VIRGO) ENVIRONMENT

If Lucky For You: The house is clean and orderly. Cooking i:
methodical - everything is measured precisely. A mess is cleane
up immediately - neatness prevails. Work is brought home fror
the office; you enjoy laboring in this environment. You manag
to read, write and study in between chores. The atmosphere i:
quiet and peaceful. Entertainment is infrequent. Only a few guest
at a time are desired. Those who are intelligent are the mos
sought after. Knowledge is of utmost importance. Stimulatin,
conversations keep your mind alert. Time is not wasted o:
frivolous things such as pranks. Games and sports are not tha
popular in this environment. Mental activities reign.

In the office, you are an overachiever. You are efficien
fastidious and pay close attention to detail. Excellent plans ar
made and kept. You can easily see the flaws in the ideas of others
People value your opinion. The place is quiet and it is easy t
concentrate here. Co-workers are polite. In this atmosphere, yo
do not talk much unless it pertains to business. It seems that al
you want to do is work - work - work.

If Unlucky For You: If everything is not in order, you fuss an
fuss and fuss. You, or others, are picky and critical to a fault
There are many distractions. It is difficult to finish your tasks
Your nerves are jangled and on edge. You can't seem t
concentrate on your job due to the noise: talk, gossip, machinery
office equipment, phones ringing, repairmen shouting, and so on
The office is messy; things are disorganized and that bothers you
Confusion reigns. Misunderstandings develop. Communicatio:
is a problem.

Your guests may feel uncomfortable when you entertain
because you clean the ashtray after each use. Meals have to b
served on schedule; thus, drinks are few and timed so as not t
interfere with dinner. The table is set with the proper napkins

glasses, silverware and dishes for the occasion. You expect others to have good manners and know etiquette. Once alone, you spend most of your time cleaning the house. Everything is put in such perfect order that the other members of your household cannot find their belongings. Your criticism, when others arrive home late for dinner, is annoying. You are difficult to live with because you are such a perfectionist and expect others to be the same.

A NUMBER 3 (LIBRA) OR NUMBER 6 (VENUS) ENVIRONMENT

If Lucky For You: The home is beautifully decorated and resembles those seen in magazines depicting the lifestyle of the rich and famous. Peace and harmony prevail. Entertaining is a must. The social urges are dominant, regardless of whether it is in your abode or somewhere else - restaurant, nightclub, country club or the home of a client, friend, associate or acquaintance. The guests invited to your house are elegant, friendly, kind, charming and have good manners. Your personality wins others over to your side. Intellectual conversations reign. The environment is artistic and romantic. Soft music and lights, candlelit suppers and tender loving moments are experienced. Affection is expressed openly. It is a warm, cozy and very pleasant atmosphere. Everyone in congenial.

The office is quiet, except when parties are given. However, there is never any rowdiness in this atmosphere. It is popular place where others visit on business or make social calls that wind up in financial ventures. Gifts are readily given to those who work in this environment. Presents are bestowed by outsiders or co-workers. Salary increases augment your income. Promotions give prestige. A true brotherhood spirit exists because everyone tries to help each other. Profits roll in easily. Plenty of sweets may be

61

eaten in this office. Your charming personality makes the place sparkle. Bosses and co-workers are kind and gentle.

If Unlucky For You: Indecisiveness may cause a deal to be lost. Your laziness hinders pay raises and advances in position. There is a tendency to take the easy way out. In this atmosphere, you energy level may be low. A tendency to goof off could make you lose your job, especially if you prolong those lunches and continue to be late to work to take too much time off.

In this home environment, it is difficult to make up your mind when it comes to many things, especially with what clothes you should wear. Your family calls you shiftless, but, due to your charm, those close to you do not reprimand you for being lackadaisical. You enjoy relaxing in the home; however, as a result, it is not easy to accomplish ordinary tasks. Often, you take the line of least resistance when decisions have to be made. One moment you want to change the decor, but a few minutes later you change your mind. Or your are perhaps toying with the idea of entertaining. But, then again, that takes a lot of effort - sometimes more than you care to expend. There are times when you just sit still and do not want to do anything. Your home is attractively furnished, although some colors may be mismatched a little; this doesn't disturb you, but may bother a professional decorator.

In this atmosphere, a desire to be loved is strong. Romance is uppermost in you mind most of the time. Love affairs may go sour and can be very hurting. You are extremely sensitive and emotional in this atmosphere - and just can't seem to help yourself.

A NUMBER 4 (SCORPIO) OR 22 (PLUTO) ENVIRONMENT
If Lucky For You: The house is orderly and immaculate. Small groups, or just the two of you, are preferable when entertaining. Many productive tasks are accomplished due to a strong creative

drive. A loved one is treasured and given your undivided attention. Privacy is desired when you are living with the person you adore. It's easy to be reclusive in this atmosphere and to watch television a lot. If you are with a partner, there's an abundance of sex. Everyone is cooperative, and teamwork reigns. The air seems to be filled with energy.

It is easy to concentrate in your working environment. All projects are accomplished quickly and efficiently. A tremendous amount of labor is expended. If you are an employee, the boss is pleased with your work; thus, it does not take you long to reach the top. However, if you are the owner of the business, expect to expand it in this atmosphere. Your ability to get everyone to cooperate with your plans makes for success.

If Unlucky For You: There is a tendency to hibernate and not entertain much. You may brook and be in some dark moods. Jealous scenes with violent fights take place, especially if you try to smother a loved one. Deep resentments fester and break wide open with a stormy battle that may last through the night. You may be bitchy and temperamental. Your loved one may feel like a prisoner, especially when you refuse to open your door to visitors, including relatives and in-laws. Theft and danger are more easily attracted in a number 22 vibration than any other number vibration! If none of the foregoing is attracted, then it's possible that you attract accidents in your home - burn or cut yourself, drop and spill things or bump into furniture, and so on. It's a hectic and rushed atmosphere that makes you easily aroused to anger.

In the office, jealousies and resentments prevail. You may want to get even with those who are disloyal, bitchy, nasty or mean. Losses in business could occur because bitter enemies are made. You want control. You do not trust anyone. Every action anyone

takes is noticed by you. You may refuse to cooperate with others,
preferring to work alone. Stubbornness and resistance to change
could cause financial difficulties. Deadlines and pressures cause
such stress and tension that the entire office staff may appear as
though they are ready to erupt like a volcano. It is an angry
environment. Accidents on the job occur. Mechanical devices
break down. Everyone is in such a rush that tempers fly and
disagreements are attracted.

A NUMBER 5 (JUPITER) OR NUMBER 7 (SAGITTARIUS) ENVIRONMENT

If Lucky For You: The house is filled with expensive items or
with art objects, paintings, plants and large furniture. The rooms
are grand and spacious. It is a joyous atmosphere with laughter
filling the air. Pranks are played upon others with a spirit of give
and take. Philosophical themes are bantered about. It may be a
religious environment with artifacts, a bible or rosary - prayers
may be said daily. Everyone seems happy, and the place always
seems to be filled with visitors. Guests are treated like royalty -
pampered and waited on. Entertaining is extravagantly done - no
expense is spared. Jokes are told. Games are played, such as
monopoly, dominoes, darts, billiards, Ping Pong and Trivial
Pursuit. If the preceding doesn't fit because you are in a financial
bind, a home which vibrates to a number 5 or 7 can give you
divine protection and, at the last moment, you may be pulled out
of debt and monetary problems. This is an optimistic atmosphere
that gives confidence and a winning spirit.

In the office, you are sure of yourself and business. Everything
is on the increase. Ventures grow fast - large-scale operations
become a necessity. Expansion continues as the dollars pour in.

It is a busy place with happy vibes. People are kind to each other and go out of their way to help one another. Everyone is courteous and optimistic. The boss is generous with bonuses and pay raises that come quite steadily. It is easy to advance to high positions - promotions are granted easily. It is a "share the wealth" environment.

If Unlucky For You: Sloppiness prevails in the home. It is easy to make a mess because you couldn't care less. You may be wasteful with food, throwing leftovers out or cooking enough for an army. You give your possessions away because you are bored with them. Everything is done to excess, which may cost you a fortune. However, your happy-go-lucky attitude makes you laugh all folly right out of your life. You take others for granted and play pranks on them constantly. You frolic - and are the life of the party. It's as if you are on a merry-go-round and can't, or don't want to, get off.

You are too sure of yourself in the office. Mistakes are made, but you don't care. You may goof off. This is an atmosphere filled with laughter, jokes, bantered about and lots of fun-filled moments. Desires are difficult to realize because your goals are set too high. Others encourage you to such an extent that you take on endeavors that are not practical. Your hopes soar to the heights; thus, business may be expanded at the wrong time which may prove to be quite costly to your bank account. Your generosity could hold you back from making a profit. But, regardless of the actions you take, you will always be saved at the last moment.

A NUMBER 6 (VENUS) ENVIRONMENT (see page 61)
A NUMBER 7 (SAGITTARIUS) ENVIRONMENT (see page 64)

A NUMBER 8 (CAPRICORN) OR NUMBER 16 (SATURN) ENVIRONMENT

If Lucky For You: You can get by with the bare necessities in the home. You don't like clutter - however, you dislike throwing out things that could be useful at some future date. You can live in small quarters - practicality reigns. The house may be cold. Old or antique furnishings may be to your liking. The place is neat, tidy and orderly. The atmosphere is serious, stern, rigid. You are a disciplinarian - rules and regulations may be posted and must be obeyed. Your movements are slow, deliberate and your time is not wasted. Work may be brought home from the office. Entertaining is kept to a minimum because you enjoy being thrifty and having money in the bank. You could live on a fixed income. You don't spend much on food. It is difficult to move from this abode - you don't budge.

The office environment is similar to your home - staid, proper, strict and respectable. Excellent decisions and plans are made. You are observant and nothing gets by you. Your ambitions may take you to the pinnacle of success. You can patiently wait for your ideas to bear fruit. There are long hours put in with lots of overtime. The desire for security is strong. Every dime made is well earned and may be at the sacrifice of something personal. You are calm, cool and collected. Your desire for perfection shows in your work. You are persistent in the attainment of your goals.

If Unlucky For You: The home atmosphere is filled with so many negative thoughts that you make your life, and those of others, miserable. You are a pessimist. There is a tendency to gripe and complain every time things do not go your way. You could be a nag. There is coldness in the air that has nothing to do with the temperature. You are too serious, seldom cracking a smile. It seems as though you are filled with self-pity. Poverty-like conditions can be attracted. A loneliness sets in and you may feel unloved and rejected by the world. In your silence, the tears may echo through the rooms as you sob bitterly. You've got the blues in this environment.

In the office, you are inclined to be greedy, ambitious and may use others to get to the top. You gripe and complain if you do not get promoted or receive a salary increase. There is a tendency to blame others for your actions. Depression reigns. Losses are attracted. It is an all-work-and-no-play environment. The office may be small and cramped. You are suspicious of others, thinking that they have ulterior motives in mind. You feel trapped. You are afraid to ask for a change; thus, you sit and brood and feel sorry for yourself. You believe you are being punished.

A NUMBER 9 (AQUARIUS) OR NUMBER 10 (URANUS) ENVIRONMENT

If Lucky For You: Many happy hours are spent in the home while engaged in reading or conversing in esoteric areas-astrology, numerology, graphology, palmistry or any subject that is off the beaten path. Intellectuality reigns. A deep interest in psychology prevails. The mysteries of the mind are probed. You do things spontaneously - like suddenly deciding to throw a party. Your friends are many and fill the room. You are not home much - it's an in and out situation. The telephone rings and "out" you go. You must have freedom to come and go as you please. You don't want to be tied down. Phone conversations are quick and to the point. Your pals drop by without calling - they are welcome any time. Interesting disruptions occur. There are not many dull moments. Your love life is a fascinating and mind-boggling experience. You may be mesmerized by those you live with. Romance may be on a high mental level.

In the office, freedom and independence are needed just as much as in the home environment. There is constant excitement and the air seems to be filled with electricity. It is a hectic work schedule. You may have to stay late and put in a lot of overtime. Unusual and inventive ideas are profitable. New products and projects captivate your interest. Avant-garde propositions and innovative methods pay off. You are in advance of the times and are interested in the latest devices and equipment which, when put into use, reap great profits. Modernization is your aim, and the quickest way of performing a job is a must. Short-cut methods are put into practice constantly. Money is quickly earned and your magnetic personality brings you many clients and friends.

If Unlucky For You: The light bulbs go out and the electrical appliances go on the blink almost daily. People drop by unexpectedly, which is upsetting. There is constant chaos at every moment; one shock after another. A sudden urge to entertain may be costly, especially when others cancel at the last moment, fail to show up or play crazy pranks on you. The house may be topsy turvy as you search for an item. The furniture doesn't match, or if it does, you don't finish decorating your home. Things are left undone. There is one disruption after another. It's difficult to make plans in this environment because, if you do, they may not take place.

In the office, the computer and electronic devices are out of order most of the time. Sudden changes of plans occur on the job. You never know what to expect from moment to moment. You may have to work overtime - and the boss may forget to pay you for it. Conditions are erratic and unstable, and anything is likely to happen. You may deal, or work, with crazy and eccentric people. There is a tendency for you to be abrupt. Sudden losses may occur - either money or a job, or you are fired, quit or walk off. Bankruptcy and transfers to other departments may occur. A strike could close down operations temporarily. The place may go bankrupt and you can't collect the money due you.

A NUMBER 11 (NEPTUNE) OR NUMBER 12 (PISCES) ENVIRONMENT

If Lucky For You: Your house is dramatic like a stage setting. There is love, warmth and comfort which makes you desirable company. A tendency to be poetical, romantic and sentimental, and to listen to dreamy and beautiful music. The depths of your soul are stirred by the beauty of these things, as well as love. There is an interest in mystical subjects and you will be quite psychic in this atmosphere - or be drawn to develop your E.S.P. A search for Utopia may make you think you have discovered it, and thus lead to a life of seclusion in this ethereal environment. Movies are watched on the VCR machine and television; perhaps you are the owner of a large screen and have a special room in which to show film. You can daydream and get lazy in this environment. It is easy to procrastinate, even when these are lucky number vibrations.

In the office, business booms due to your ballyhoo tactics. You can wheel and deal. All projects are promoted with ease. Your ideas for expansion are stupendous and, if made practical, could make you and others rich. You could turn fantasy dreams into a real fortune. You do everything on a grand scale; you often have to charm others so they will go along with your fantastic plans. Your visions could be profitable.

If Unlucky For You: In the home, you escape to the world of film or live in your daydream world where everything you imagine seems real. If others are around, they have to be careful of their conversations; your feelings are easily hurt, and even the wrong tone of voice can make you cry. Lies are told, exaggerations are made and distortions seem to be a daily habit. You procrastinate with the household chores. Clothes may be found on the floor, on a chair or on the sofa. You are a giver, and often get taken due to your gullible nature. It is easy for you to fall hook, line and sinker for a sob story. The loved one is worshiped. Deception may occur. Later, you wake up to reality and wonder how you could have been so madly in love. Your mind seems to be in the clouds and you can become forgetful - absentmindedness reigns.

Mistakes, such as transposing figures, are made in the office because you tend to daydream. You are thinking about Shangri-la. Putting off projects could cost you a job or a good financial deal. Phony schemes are attracted; propositions fail, fizzle, fall through or are not as represented. Deception is the name of the game. Losses are attracted due to sheer laziness. There is a tendency to be impractical. It is difficult to face reality - the dreams are big and so are the disappointments.

A NUMBER 13 (ARIES) OR NUMBER 16 (MARS) ENVIRONMENT

If Lucky For You: The house is cleaned fast, the dishes are done in a jiffy and you may run from room to room. You're always in a rush. It is possible you may not be home much. Entertaining is casual. Telephone conversations are quick. Sex in increased and very fiery. In this environment, you'll get up on ladders, paint ceilings and hang things that require skill. You're gutsy and courageous in your residence. You may be handy with tools and fix things that need repairing - you'll give it a whirl even though you've never previously attempted these tasks.

In the office, the initiative is taken, deals are pushed and chances do seem risky. You''ve got nerve - a pioneering and competitive spirit prevails. It is a rush - rush - rush atmosphere. The pace is fast, conversations are hurried, and creative endeavors may have top priority. You may find yourself extremely enterprising. You will go where angels fear to tread. Aggressive action is taken. New equipment is bought on the spur of the moment; decisions along these lines are beneficial in the end. It is difficult to sit still. The goal may be to accomplish the seemingly impossible. And you just might!

If Unlucky For You: In the home or office, a tense atmosphere can be expected. Arguments and constant clashes may be the order of the day. Risks, which cause losses, are taken. A tendency of being too gutsy exists. Frankness in voicing opinions may cause you to get into plenty of hot water with others. Competitiveness to outdo everyone may lead to jealous and stormy scenes. The place may be in an uproar. Accidents take place - burns, cuts, bruises from bumping into furniture. You may knock down art objects. You are in such a hurry that you spill food. Anger is aroused quickly. Or, fights could be a daily occurrence. You are quick to take offense. You leap into things without first thinking them through. Details are overlooked. You are extremely impatient.

A NUMBER 14 (TAURUS) ENVIRONMENT

If Lucky For You: Peace, quiet and harmony prevail in the home. Classical music may be played on a tape deck, or you may listen to the latest "in" C.D.'s. The house is decorated beautifully with lots of plants and flowers. It is a warm and comfortable place.

71

The yard may be landscaped - a blooming and colorful garden looks like a magazine cover. You may find that you have a green thumb in this environment. You are a little stubborn, yet pleasant and easy to get along with. You may not want anyone to move or change the furniture. Your charming personality is shown when you entertain graciously. You enjoy the social scene. Food is either served elegantly in a formal dining room or casually as a buffet. Your guests dress for the occasion. Everyone seems well mannered. A loved one is wined and dined - it's a romantic place. Sex is a very sensual experience.

In the office, efficiency prevails and deals are made slowly because you want to be sure you are making the right decisions. Everything is scrutinized carefully before any action is taken. The place is neat, tidy and orderly, and the abundance of growing plants makes it quite attractive. The pace is slow; the environment is non-competitive. Money is made, but you don't rush to spend it. You tend to be thrifty. Office equipment and supplies are purchased only when deemed necessary. You'll buy the latest "in" electronic machinery or computer equipment and software if you are confident that these purchases will speed up production and increase your profits.

If Unlucky For You: Stubbornness prevails to the extend that you may lock horns with those in the home or office - especially when they suggest making changes. If they attempt to move the furniture or art objects, your anger may shock them. In this atmosphere, it takes you a while to be aroused, but, once the boiling point is reached, others should be ready for the explosion. Most of the time peace and harmony reign, but you do have your off-moments when others rub you the wrong way. Your actions are slow. Deals seem to take forever to be consummated. If you are the boss, or the head of the household, your conservativeness may be taken as miserliness. If you are employed in this number 14 environment, your superior may be too thrifty and not give you the type of raises you think you deserve. As a result, you may stay employed here and sulk over your misfortune. The desire to have a secure job could make you afraid to chance looking elsewhere. Thus, you may find yourself in a rut that's difficult to change.

A NUMBER 15 (SATURN) ENVIRONMENT (see page 66)
A NUMBER 16 (MARS) ENVIRONMENT (see page 70)
A NUMBER 17 (GEMINI) ENVIRONMENT (see page 58)

A NUMBER 18 (CANCER) OR NUMBER 20 (MOON) ENVIRONMENT

If Lucky For You: The refrigerator and cabinet shelves are stocked with food. Every type of pan and pot imaginable is either hung up on a wall or tucked away in storage cabinets. Special dishes for escargot, parfaits or seafood appetizers are neatly stored. Shells, baskets, and special corn asparagus dishes are on the shelves. This is a domestic environment - the desire to cook and eat tasty food dominates the scene. The place may seem cluttered with knick-knacks. The rooms are cozy and comfortable. The kitchen wall may have a hanging sign that reads *Home Sweet Home*. There are quilts, plants, flowers, needlepoint pillows, and other hand-sewn items; perhaps there is a braided rug on the floor in front of the fireplace. There is a lot of love and warmth in this house. Friends are entertained and relatives visit constantly. It is a relaxed environment that makes one move slowly and enjoy every moment is this abode.

In the office, the action is slightly retarded - mistakes are avoided. Chances are not taken. The work gets done efficiently. There is old-fashioned equipment interspersed with modern machinery. Everyone seems to be warm and kind. A sympathetic and helpful atmosphere prevails. The desire to be needed is strong. In this office number 18 or number 20, you and those you deal with are easygoing. Food is brought in and eaten. It seems that everyone has a healthy appetite in this environment. It's as if the crew and bosses are a large and happy family working together for a mutual and beneficial cause. If you are employed here, you are satisfied with pay raises; if you own the business, the profits keep you smiling all the way to the bank.

If Unlucky For You: Your emotions are out of control. Tears flow easily and enough to fill a few buckets. It is difficult to stop crying. It seems as if your feelings get hurt every time you turn around. Thus, a shell is crawled into and not a word is spoken for days. The pace is slow. Upsets could put you into a bad mood so the house doesn't get cleaned. A food binge is indulged in when your are frustrated. Dishes are left in the sink. Your place may resemble a pig's pen. The mess is so bad that you just can't seem to cope with it. If you are looking for something, you get annoyed because the clutter is more than you can bear. Objects are thrown into closets and kept for sentimental reasons. Emotional tizzies are thrown when something can't be found. Yours is a house that seems as if a tornado has hit - especially when you are out of sorts.

Food is brought to the office and the drawers are stuffed with snacks. It is easy to gain weight in this atmosphere. It takes forever to accomplish a task, especially if upsets that lead to frustration block the way to finish a job. Your emotions are at an all-time high. It is difficult for you to handle tasks and problems, especially when you are moody and changeable. Decisions do not come easily when made and losses could result. You may not accomplish all the tasks at hand; projects may be abandoned in midstream due to boredom setting in. Gossip abounds. Ups and owns are experienced when dealing with clients or the public. Co-workers could put you into a tearful mood. Office equipment may be old-fashioned and need to be updated, but you can't make up your mind as to what type of new machinery you should buy or lease.

NUMBER 19 (LEO) OR NUMBER 21 (SUN) ENVIRONMENT

If Lucky For You: Home is like a show place; regal with expensive furnishings. Or, if you don't have a lot of money, you have a few elegant objects set in a tasteful decor. If you are wealthy, entertainment is lavish and guests may be famous, in powerful positions, belong to royalty or be successful entrepreneurs. If you are in a low income bracket, you may invite the boss over for dinner and go out of your way to give the best service you can afford. In fact, you could live beyond your means in this atmosphere. Compliments are received on your home, and your ego soars because you are proud of the way you have decorated the place. This environment gives off a feeling of stability. You rule the house with kindness and firmness. It is a home filled with love.

In the office, deals seem to flourish due to hard work. You could be in a prestigious position or own your own business. Pay raises and promotions come easily and often. Those in authoritative positions favor you and go out of their way to grant you most of your wishes. Praises are bestowed which inflate your ego, but not to the extent to make you lord it over others. The office runs smoothly with hardly any mishaps. You take pride in the efficient way things are handled. You want the best computers, office and equipment and machinery that is available, regardless of the cost. You don't hesitate to buy the latest models.

75

Large-scale operation is a must. Petty things bore you ... everything must be big - deals, contracts, publicity, and the number of employees. You could be a financial giant in this location.

If Unlucky For You: Difficulties occur with others due to bragging. If you are the boss, employees are lost because you are an egomaniac. In fact, your ego is your downfall. If you are employed in this location, problems occur with people in authority. You desire center stage; but, if it cannot be had, your actions may cause others to dislike you. It is difficult to obtain pay raises and promotions. You could attract losses through overextending yourself with equipment that is not needed. Perhaps you purchased it just for show. To impress people here is a must, and that could be very costly. You and others are too bossy in this atmosphere.

The home may be ostentatious and all entertaining is done in a flamboyant fashion, even if you can't afford it. The family, as well as outsiders, think that you are a snob or just too authoritative. You are stubborn. You rule the roost to such an extent others are miserable. It seems that you are never pleased by their actions because they are not as perfect as you; thus, problems are constantly attracted. Your desire for order, neatness and perfection could disturb your family and guests.

A NUMBER 20 (MOON) ENVIRONMENT (see page 73)
A NUMBER 21 (SUN) ENVIRONMENT (see page 75)
A NUMBER 22 (PLUTO) ENVIRONMENT (see page 62)

Do you know there is a right and wrong time to gamble? Everything is in the time. Don't waste your money gambling on wrong astrological dates. Lynne Palmer's *__Gambling To Win__* has easy to use instructions on how to pick your best dates to win. Also learn how to play table games (craps, blackjack etc.), video poker and other games of chance. *Hot tips* are given. Don't wait another minute! Order *GAMBLING TO WIN.*

Send to: Star Bright Publishers
               2235 East Flamingo Road, Suite 300-D
               Las Vegas, NV 89119
   Make check or money order (no C.O.D.'s)
   Note: Nevada residents, add 7% State Sales Tax
☐ I enclose $14.95 *(includes shipping/handling)*
for *GAMBLING TO WIN.*

Name _____

Address _____

City _____ State _____ Zip _____
   Price and postage subject to change

Lynne Palmer's book *MONEY MAGIC* contains secrets for prosperity and Money Magical Devices not found in print anywhere else.

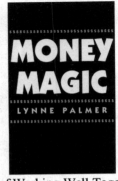

Learn how to harness power that could make you wealthy.

The Luck that leads to Affluence The Chemistry of Working Well Together

And the Magic that makes MILLIONS-----you'll find them all in *MONEY MAGIC.*

Send to: Star Bright Publishers.

2235 East Flamingo Road, Suite 300-D

Las Vegas, NV 89119

Make check or money order (no C.O.D.'s)

<u>Note:</u> *Nevada residents, add 7% State Sales Tax*

☐ I enclose $12.00 *(includes shipping/handling)* for *MONEY MAGIC.*

Name _____

Address _____

City _____ State _____ Zip _____

Price and postage subject to change

How would you like to own a mental and visual aid that could help make your wishes/dreams come true? Take action! Order your own *A s t r o l o g i c a l Treasure Map* which comes with easy-to-use instructions. Your life could change in 3 months! Why not have it all?

Love, money, happiness, business success and so on can be yours. Start now and pave the road to riches by ordering Lynne Palmer's booklet *the ASTROLOGICAL TREASURE MAP*.

Send to: Star Bright Publishers.

2235 East Flamingo Road, Suite 300-D
Las Vegas, NV 89119

Make check or money order (no C.O.D.'s)
Note: Nevada residents, add 7% State Sales Tax

☐ I enclose $12.95 *(includes shipping/handling)* for the *Astrological Treasure Map.*

Name _____

Address _____

City _____ State _____ Zip _____

Birthdate _____

Place of Birth

Time of Birth

Price and postage subject to change

For as little as $1.50 per month you'll be able to plan your life day-by-day with Lynne Palmer's **ASTROLOGICAL ALMANAC.**

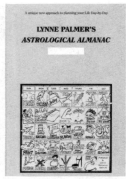

Merely look up any of the 464 categories listed; then plan ahead for the best day to do whatever you choose from **A** (Advertising) to **Y** (Yoga).

Move. Date. Marry. Open a business. Start a diet. Have surgery, dental work or legal action. Avoid travel by air on bad dates. Plus *Your Sun Sign Yearly Forecast*, places to live, climate, color, gifts, perfume and so much more.

Send to: Star Bright Publishers.

2235 East Flamingo Road, Suite 300-D
Las Vegas, NV 89119

Make check or money order (no C.O.D.'s)

<u>Note:</u> *Nevada residents, add 7% State Sales Tax*

☐ I enclose $23.00 *(includes shipping/handling)* for the *ASTROLOGICAL ALMANAC.*

Name ————————————————————

Address ————————————————————

City ——————————— State ——— Zip ———

Price and postage subject to change